Building Sustainability in the Balance:
Promoting Stakeholder Dialogue

By

Sarah Sayce
Anthony Walker
Angus McIntosh

2004

A division of Reed Business Information

Estates Gazette, 151 Wardour Street, London W1F 8BN

ISBN 0 7282 0424 X

Typeset by Amy Boyle, Rochester, Kent
Printed by Interprint, Malta

Contents

List of Boxes, Figures, Tables and Illustrations

Boxes

Figures

Tables

Illustrations

Acknowledgements

Throughout the preparation of this book and the research project which proceeded it the authors have constantly been grateful for the vast body of interest in the topic of sustainability and the enormous support which they have received both directly and indirectly by comments, information or even just through access to published and unpublished work.

In particular we would like to thank those who have given time and advice through the advisory group to the research project John Anderson, Jerry Barford, John Doggart, Anthony Holmes, Hugh Seigle, Phil Shearer, Andrew Wilson, and our researcher Jo Koenig. We would also like to thank the government bodies, initially the DETR and subsequently the DTI, for their support and particularly Dr Mervyn Jones who as their representative gave unstinting and valuable advice.

Our thanks would not be complete without mention of our families who put up with, and often gave assistance in, the compilation of both research and the present book and of course our respective organisations, Kingston University, DLG Architects and King Sturge where we hope we may have fired an enthusiasm for a real understanding of Sustainability.

The real reward for us all lies in the future and we hope that through the work which has gone into this project, the awareness which it has helped to engender and the understanding of the conflicts inherent in some of the interests we will have helped to make sure that sustainability will no longer be an issue for our children and our children's children. Our present lays the foundation for their future.

Preface

> '*Study how a society uses land, and you can come to pretty reliable conclusions as to what its future will be*' (Schumacher, 1973:93)

By way of introduction

The aim of this book is to provide a signpost guide for architects and designers, planners, property occupiers, owners and their consultants so that they may be better informed in making decisions about the future life of a building and in particular about whether or not a building should survive. Many publications have concentrated on the technical issues of environmental sustainability or sought, through sustainability accounting, to take note of the internal and external interests in a building. Few however have sought to identify the conflicts of interest which need to be resolved in order to discover the future prospects of a building.

Here the interests of the different stakeholders are identified, the key issues over which they may be in conflict are considered and discussed, and the Building Sustainability Assessment Tool (BSAT detailed in Chapter 6) is proposed to provide a framework for constructive dialogue between any number of participants.

Decisions regarding the re-use or redevelopment of buildings are driven primarily by a simple economic agenda which may be tempered by the constraints of planning and building regulations. The economic requirements of building owners and occupiers have often been in conflict with those of the community and until now the only protection has been through listing or the creation of special planning status, such as a designated conservation area. Listing is the most specific protection and this is applied only where a building

has been recognised as having a special value to the community, both present and future. The criteria used in determining whether a building should be listed are restricted to special architectural or historic interest and its wider socio-economic 'value' is not specifically recognised.

Our argument is that such simple decision making is no longer appropriate. The increasing acceptance of sustainability principles within the UK and most other developed nation states has changed the parameters irrevocably; legislation, in the form of social and environmental agendas, is having a significant impact on building design through changes to building regulations, but its impact goes far beyond this. Both occupiers and investors are increasingly recognising that Corporate Social Responsibility (CSR) pervades not just their business policies but also their property portfolios. Socially Responsible Investment (SRI) as a means for investors to demonstrate their adherence to CSR policies, is becoming a common policy among major property owners and investors.

Inevitably, moving to a new, more inclusive decision-making process is difficult. The principles of sustainability are not yet universally accepted nor are they fully understood even at the most general level and the application of this concept to practical decisions will not be easy. That however is no reason for inaction and it is only through debate and dialogue that progress will be made.

It is therefore vitally important that all those concerned with the built environment should develop a full understanding of the issues. Much of the research and advice published so far quantifies the issues so that a building's fate may be measured according to specific factors. Such an approach can be misleading. Measuring sustainability is not an exact science and attempts to confine decisions within a mathematical framework may be more misleading than helpful; as Bell and Morse (1999) argue, indicators of sustainability are about measuring the immeasurable!

This book is a reaction to increasing reliance on measurable criteria to drive decision making. Quality issues are by definition largely subjective and of far greater practical importance in creating and maintaining a viable and appropriate future life for a building or in determining that it is ripe for redevelopment, than those for which factual measurement can be made.

This was one of the main findings of the project funded by the DTI, *Buildings: a new life*, on which

this book is based and which is summarised in Appendix A. It provides an introduction to the issues and presents a schematic tool for use in the evaluation of existing commercial buildings. The ambition of the authors is that the book and the BSAT may provide the means for real communication between the stakeholders when making decisions about the future life or death of a commercial building.

While the focus here is on commercial buildings many of the issues apply equally to non-commercial stock. It is recognised that the regeneration of a building often implies a change of use. The original purpose may well be superseded by a new economic or social demand very different from that originally anticipated. For example one of the case studies considered in the project, the Rodboro Buildings in Guildford, Surrey, originated in the early 20th century as a car production unit but at the

Rodboro Buildings, Guildford circa 1990 The Rodboro Buildings in Guildford were one of the case studies undertaken by the authors as part of the *Buildings: a new life* research project.

time of writing it has found a new life as a public house and dance studio.

The book is in six chapters with four appendices comprising a summary of the research programme *Buildings: a new life*, a glossary, bibliography and formula for the proposed assessment tool.

In Chapter 1 the principles and conflicts inherent in sustainability are considered. In Chapters 2 to 4 we examine the topic from the 'triple bottom line' interests of economic, environmental and social sustainability and in Chapter 5 we consider the different stakeholders and their specific interests. Each chapter starts with an outline of the issues to be considered which is then related to the built environment and thus to the individual building concluding with a summary of issues affecting future building use.

Chapter 6 reflects on the issues considered and presents the Building Sustainability Assessment Tool (BSAT). This provides a framework whereby a building can be scored from different stakeholder perspectives against differing sustainability criteria.

The guide is generic: its purpose is to stimulate discussion, not to provide a firm definitive and quantitative solution for each set of circumstances which is neither feasible nor desirable.

All buildings present an individual case but this analysis applies to a greater or lesser extent to all commercial properties. BSAT therefore allows the users to make adjustments to incorporate additional characteristics and to adjust the weighting given to individual decision criteria.

In recognition of the need to explore each aspect further before reaching a score for each item, a guide to references and further reading is included as an Appendix which will provide the reader with the detail technical information which is outside the objectives of this book.

Sarah Sayce
Anthony Walker
Angus McIntosh

London 2003

Chapter 1

Introduction: Principles and Conflicts

Principal Messages:

- *The concept of sustainable development has been widely adopted by governments across the world and it is an important part of both EU and UK policy. It is it based on a principle of intergenerational equity.*
- *Legislation is increasingly being brought forward both to encourage and to coerce the property and construction industry, from designers to eventual investors, to adopt its principles.*
- *This means far more than designing new energy-efficient buildings.*
- *It means appropriate conservation of existing stock and acceptance of an approach to building management and maintenance that balances economic, environmental and social concerns.*
- *Decisions affecting individual buildings will often be difficult. An informed dialogue between stakeholders is required to ensure that the principles of sustainability can be incorporated into decisions that affect not just new buildings but the future lives of existing stock.*

The concept of sustainable development

The concept of sustainable development sets great challenges for everyone and in recent times a combination of governmental legislation, political pressures and an increased awareness on the part of the public, places the onus on all professional people to conduct their businesses in such a way that it does not conflict with the ambition of UK government to promote sustainable development.

Sustainable development affects everybody, but it has a special relevance to all those concerned with the creation and maintenance of the built environment: our towns and cities and the buildings that create them. UK government, in line with EU policy, espouses the promotion of 'sustainable construction' with the ambition that, over time, the total building stock will be more sustainable. The essence of sustainable development requires that, in all development activity, due account is taken of both the short and long term of the activity for all

those affected. Those affected include people across both space (i.e. including those in other countries) and time (i.e. subsequent generations).

All professionals in this field have a unique opportunity and obligation to promote the concept of sustainable development, whether they are planning advisers, architects or contractors concerned with the construction process, building surveyors, agents or investment owners concerned with the management and performance of properties during any period of their life cycle.

One of the key decisions for buildings that has implications for sustainable development is whether to demolish or retain an existing building. Economically, the decision may seem relatively simple but if the principles of sustainable development are to be adopted, the implications become more complex.

This guide has been produced to raise awareness among professionals of some of the issues that affect the assessment of an existing building in sustainability terms. In particular, the Building Sustainability Assessment Tool (BSAT) (see Chapter 6) is designed to help identify the key areas in which disagreement is likely to occur between the various different stakeholders. It is a fundamental premise of the book that conflict is inevitable and this is supported by the research. It is also a premise that appropriate resolution should be the ambition of all those concerned. The Tool provides a framework within which the future life of a building can be evaluated in order to assist stakeholders to make appropriate decisions; it is intended that it may be of use primarily when a decision to either demolish or refurbish is contemplated. Neither the Tool nor the book seeks to advocate retention of a building in every case; rather the intention is that decisions are taken within a wider context and after informed discussion.

A definition of sustainable development

There is no one universally accepted definition of sustainable development. Most commonly adopted is the Bruntland definition: '*Sustainable Development means the ability to meet our own needs without prejudicing the ability of future generations to meet their own needs*' (World Commission on Environment and Development, 1987).

Sustainable development has become a watchword for many governments, over the last decade of the 20th century, following the Rio declaration in 1992. At this summit meeting governments across many parts of the globe signed up to a set of principles and actions at international, national and local level. A key part of this global alliance was that countries should act at the local level in order to achieve global ambitions. The global agenda is essentially simple and enshrines a set of eight main principles that governments should ensure:

- The fundamental right of all human beings to an environment that is adequate for their heath and well-being;
- The conservation and proper use of the environment (including built environment) in a way that benefits current and future generations;
- The promotion of bio-diversity to ensure ecosystem maintenance;
- The monitoring of environmental standards and publication of data related thereto;
- The prior assessment of environmental impacts of significant developments;
- That all individuals are informed of planned activities and given rights to justice;
- That conservation is integral to the planning and implementation of development activities; and
- That they should co-operate with other states towards mutual implementation.

The eight principles have been, and increasingly are being, enshrined in legislation at the transnational (European Union [EU]) and national (United Kingdom [UK]) level and through the promotion of local measures by local government through Agenda 21.

Box 1.1: Agenda 21: A definition

Agenda 21 is a 300-page plan for achieving sustainable development in the 21st century. Developed by the Commission on Sustainable Development following the Rio Summit in 1992, Agenda 21 is a comprehensive plan of action designed to be adopted at every level of government: global, national and local by organisations of the United Nations System, Governments, and Major Groups in every area in which human impacts on the environment. It seeks to address 'the pressing problems of today and also aims at preparing the world for the challenges of the next century. It reflects a global consensus and political commitment at the highest level on development and environment co-operation. Its successful implementation is first and foremost the responsibility of Governments. National strategies, plans, policies and processes are crucial in achieving this. International co-operation should support and supplement such national efforts. In this context, the United Nations system has a key role to play. Other international, regional and sub-regional organisations are also called upon to contribute to this effort. The broadest public participation and the active involvement of the non-governmental organisations and other groups should also be encouraged.' (www.un.org)

A significant number of local authorities are incorporating Agenda 21 in their policies (1) and are requiring developers to make statements in respect of the Agenda in major applications at least. This means that all those involved with the development or redevelopment process must be not only knowledgeable about such matters but also able to interpret policy in practical terms.

In addition, other legislation relating to sustainability also affects the built environment. It is not just through the planning laws and building control (including Disabled Access legislation) that buildings are affected. They increasingly have to be designed, developed and managed so that owners and occupiers can comply with a raft of social legislation from regulation of pension funds to control of working hours. All these factors have an important bearing on which buildings will succeed over time and which will fail.

The triple bottom line principle

An examination of the eight principles of sustainable development reveals that they relate to three underlying themes:

- The promotion of environmental well-being, so that environmental degradation is minimised and natural resources are used to the greatest benefit. This implies *inter alia*:

  - the conservation of non-renewable energy resources;
  - reduction of greenhouse gas emissions;
  - promotion of use of renewable energy sources; and
  - management of resources, including waste management.

- The protection of, and proper respect for, people so that the common human condition as measured by indices such as the United Nations Human Development Index is improved, not just among the population of that nation state but internationally. This implies that government and individuals should work to ensure:

  - appropriate working conditions including their physical environment;
  - adequate care of the less advantaged including issues of access to premises;
  - social legislation to ensure good governance at all levels from government to individual organisations; and
  - that all people have appropriate opportunities in terms of education and work.

- The creation of an economic context in which sustainable development can be achieved. It is difficult to promote decisions that are in the best interests of sustainable development, be it at the government or local level, where these conflict with the economic imperative placed on stakeholders (for example the requirement to satisfy shareholder demands). Often there is a direct correlation between economic success and environmental pollution: in simple terms, the more economically successful the country, the more it pollutes (Morse, 2002).(2)

  This means that to achieve the move to sustainable social and environment contexts they must be:

  - achievable within the realms of what is economically viable;
  - acceptable to the range of different stakeholders involved in the development activity since no progress is achievable without adequate economic returns for those who promote development; and
  - capable of measurement so that appropriate 'indicators' can inform economic decision-makers.

It follows that the sustainable development agenda has three main strands, all of which need to work in harmony. These are:

- Economic,
- Environmental, and
- Social.

Activity which seeks to balance these three elements is said to comply with the principles of the triple bottom line (TBL). Increasingly, corporate bodies are adopting TBL principles in developing their business activities. This is partly in response to legislative imperatives and partly due to an increasing realisation that compliance with and promotion of social and environmental well-being is good for business.

Box 1.2: Sustainability is good for business

Solid facts to prove that the Triple Bottom Line is good for business are still hard to find - but increasingly companies are convinced that it is, as they see the progress of companies included in the FTSE4Good index (www.ftse4good.com) or the Dow Jones Sustainability Index (www.sustainability-index.com).

John McDonough, Chief executive of Carrillion Services, is quoted on their website (www.carillionplc.com) as saying after Carillion was included in the FTSE4Good Index: 'We believe there is a clear business case for sustainability that benefits Carillion, our customers, our partners, our suppliers and our stakeholder communities.'

Sir Nigel Mobbs of Slough Estates, on launching their new environmental policy was quoted as saying: 'it is of paramount importance that the Group maintains high standards of environmental practice in every aspect of its business. Such practices are beneficial to our customers, our shareholders, our employees and the communities in which we invest.' (www.sloughestates.com)

The importance of sustainable development in the property and construction industries

The need to promote sustainable buildings forms an important plank of UK government policy (see Department of the Environment, Transport and the Regions [DETR], 1999 and subsequent updates from the Construction Best Practice Programme (www.cbpp.org.uk). The findings of the *Urban Task Force* (Rogers, 1999) heralded the articulation of renewed initiatives to re-vitalise the urban stock while at the same time seeking to promote sustainable development.

There are several reasons why government is seeking to promote the sustainable development agenda to the construction and property industries. Fundamental to these is the recognition of the importance of the industry to the UK economy and the realisation that buildings are key components in the context within which all activities take place. The construction industry produces some 10% of the UK's annual GDP: if it is not in good heart there could be serious repercussions on the economic competitiveness of the country.

People in the UK spend over half of their lives inside buildings. Much of this time is at work inside office, retail or industrial buildings. In the UK, 45% of the energy generated is used to heat, cool, light and ventilate buildings (Edwards, 2001, pp.10–11). Energy efficiency is therefore a goal both economically and in minimising the use of fossil fuels, since only some 10% of energy consumption is currently from renewable resources.

It is estimated that almost 50% of carbon emissions in the UK relate to commercial buildings (Thomas, 1999; Rashleigh, 2000). The problem is not one that is restricted to the UK: in Europe as a whole the contribution to emissions is in excess of 40% (European Construction Industry Federation, 2000). Much of this relates to the fact that the existing buildings do not comply with the optimal performance of new, energy efficient stock, some of which is capable of running on little or zero energy.(3)

At face value, these facts could point to an argument for widespread replacement of existing stock with new, energy efficient buildings but this would be to ignore the issue of embodied energy within the existing structure. In addition the fact that a building is constructed to meet energy efficiency criteria is again no guarantee that it will perform to specification if the building occupiers do not operate it in accordance with its design criteria.

The concept of embodied energy is not new but it was restated by Howard (1996) as '...*the energy needed to win the raw materials, manufacture them to construction materials or products, transport them at all stages and direct them on site*'. Estimates of the proportion of energy related to construction as opposed to use over the life of a building vary from 10% or 15%, to considerably more. A clear, *prima facie*, case thus exists to prolong the life of a building in order that this initial consumption is amortised over as long a period as possible. This may be achieved through judicious use of refurbishment cycles.

The notion of a ratio of embodied energy and energy in use is appealing but can be misleading.

While in principle embodied energy is an important consideration, it is hard to be precise in terms of percentage calculations. There are two reasons for this: first, the measurement of embodied energy is not an exact science in that it includes all elements involved with winning, making, transporting and assembly and there is room for significant inaccuracy and error. Secondly, the rate per metre square will vary enormously from building to building, depending on construction form and structure, design and configuration, maintenance, management and external conditions. While for example an air-conditioned office will have a higher energy in use than one that is naturally ventilated, the way in which the plant is maintained and the individual user behaviour are important considerations and complete records are seldom available.

To enable a building to achieve a longer life may yield greater environmental benefits than reducing the energy consumed in the use of the building.

Definition of sustainable buildings

There is no easy definition of what constitutes a sustainable building and it might be argued if there were one, the sustainability guide detailed in Chapter 6 would not be needed. In recent years the emphasis has been on promoting 'green' design and energy efficiency in new buildings. Many of the examples of new green buildings have been within the owner-occupied commercial sector, although there are notable examples in many other property sectors.

Although the technology exists to design buildings that are energy efficient or even energy

Wessex Water Building, Bath
The building for Wessex Water Operations by architects Bennetts Associates has been cited as possibly one of the greenest office buildings in the UK with a commitment by all the team from project manager to landscape architect to produce a sustainable environment. It won the RICS 'Building of the Year' Award in 2002.

neutral, few new buildings achieve this (Lovett, 2001). Research has identified that there are many reasons for this some of which are based on misconceptions about cost. The greatest barriers to the creation of sustainable buildings lie in:

- The difficulty in defining precisely what constitutes a sustainable building;
- The lack of an easily recognisable business case; and
- The fragmentation of interests in the building.

The definition of a sustainable building can be taken as one that simply meets the Bruntland definition but this is not easy to apply. Instead a series of criteria have been developed based on TBL principles and known as the 6 'L's of sustainable buildings.

These six criteria developed by Sayce and others in the *Business Case for Sustainable Property* (4) promote:

- **Longevity**, to optimise the use of resources and materials over time;
- **Loose fit** construction to assist in the ability to adapt to changing contexts;
- **Locations** that minimise transport impact;
- **Low energy** consumption;
- **Likeability**, or the ability to satisfy the social and utility requirements of occupiers; and
- **Loveability**, or the ability to create a favourable emotional and aesthetic response from those who view the building within its setting.

This list may be useful in informing design briefs for new buildings, but its application does present conflicts. For example, while the building occupier may seek to achieve low energy consumption, unless there is a rental differential resulting from energy efficiency, there is no benefit to an investing owner. Similarly, a building in a sustainable location that maximises public transport links would not be in demand from those for whom private transport is a priority.

Developing the 6 'Ls' principles further

The principles behind the development of the 6 L's have been tested by empirical work undertaken as part of the *Buildings: a new life* project. The aim of this survey work, the findings and methodology of which are reproduced in Appendix A, was to establish views on what factors best enabled buildings to survive over time. Extracts from the results of the survey (see Tables 1.1 and 1.2 below) reveal that fabric durability or the quality of construction is a major factor in enhancing or promoting building life, whereas the use of system building and matters of fashion were not so important in ensuring the continuing life of the buildings.

Consideration of the lowest ranked items lends little weight to the importance of social (*loveability*) or energy efficiency (*low energy*), despite the importance these issues have in the wider context and in the government's ambition to move towards green technology.

The *Buildings: a new life* research demonstrated that the debate must go beyond the notion of energy efficiency: indeed if taken on energy grounds alone demolition is increasingly hard to justify and the case for 'green' refurbishments or 'retrofits' is convincing (Hawkens *et al.*, 1999) even if not often taken up in the UK. Buildings must however retain an ability to be used, for without this only extreme protectionism will ensure their survival and they frequently have a important role within their social setting. They are part of the grain of a settlement and add to the sense of 'place'. With the moves from industrial to 'experience' economies (Pine and Gilmore, 1999), the role of property shifts to a stage set in which culture and property intertwine (Soja, 1989) and building re-use becomes increasingly tenable socially and consequentially economically.

Further consideration of some of these factors is undertaken in later chapters, but the principal arguments are introduced below.

Longevity

Longevity and durability are linked concepts, but by themselves they do not create a sustainable building. Unless a building retains the ability to be 'fit for purpose', durability is not necessarily advantageous. Indeed if flexibility is a key consideration a structure that is temporary may be more appropriate if it can be achieved with the use of fewer materials, or if the materials are capable of re-use.

This is not the same as arguing for building preservation but if the best use is to be made of

Table 1.1: The top five issues considered most important in promoting longevity

Rank	Question
1	The building has a long term durable fabric.
2	The building is capable of adaptation to reflect the changing needs of the user.
3	The building is capable of being used in an economic way.
4	The location of the building is within a conservation area or it is listed.
5	The building is able to be adapted to new technology requirements.

The other high ranking factors relate to factors of building flexibility (*loose fit*) and *location*.

Table 1.2: The bottom five issues considered to be least important in promoting longevity

Rank	Question
27	The complexity of environmental control systems affects the survival of the building.
28	The ease of access for disabled or disadvantaged persons affects the building's chance of survival.
29	Fashion in planning types of workspace affects the long-term survival of a building.
30	The use of system building with interchangeable components enhance the chances of survival of the building.
31	Fashions in appearance and perception or viability of use by the community affects building survival.

materials and energy then the longer the period over which these use can be amortised, *prima facie*, the more sustainable will be the solution. A building that fails to meet the needs of its occupiers and is unlikely so to do in the future is clearly unsustainable and where a specific use is in mind that requires a highly individualised design, longevity that continues beyond that user may not be achievable. To this extent longevity or, more accurately, optimum life may be as much a consequence of sustainability as an indicator of it.

Loose fit

Work carried out for the *Buildings: a new life* project, confirmed the findings of others (see for example Baum, 1991 and 1994; Baum and McElhinney, 2001; Brand, 1997; Kincaid, 2002) that building flexibility and adaptability are critical for the protection of economic viability which is an integral concept within sustainability.

Buildings that can be adapted for use by other occupiers are far more likely to succeed over time. Sometimes, this adaptability factor may cross uses

and the case studies used in the research clearly demonstrate this. The Travel Inn at Euston Road, London, was originally designed as an office block in the 1960s but has proved to be successful in design terms as a hotel while the cinema in Ashford Middlesex proved incapable of economic transfer across uses. This is as much a matter of basic concept as of building technology and needs to be a part of the approach to the building project from the outset.

Location

The issue of location was found to be important in empirical work on the project which was not surprising, given the strong relationship that building location has with value. But it is perhaps too simplistic to say that location is at the root of the sustainability of buildings since like the economic context, location is not a static issue. It is one of the chief determinants of economic value – but over time, the perception or reality of a location can change. For example, London Docklands, once a dominant commercial location based on shipping, became isolated and undesirable over a lengthy period in the 20th century before re-emerging as both a commercial and residential location consequent on new infra-structure and political will expressed through a range of fiscal and other economic and social incentives. Location also is a major consideration in environmental terms which in turn may have an impact on economic sustainability.

The issue of location is inter-connected both with matters of energy use and building flexibility. In energy terms transport to and from the building by occupiers and other users or related to materials and construction can be significantly affected by location and often in opposite ways since one may benefit from public transport while the other needs ease of access for large vehicles.

Low energy

Energy efficiency is becoming increasing significant for new buildings (for example, the work of BRE); however, a body of research work (Sayce *et al.*, 2001) point to its being of minor importance with regard to the buildings sustainability. Currently embodied energy is rarely taken into account in deciding a buildings fate although in a full life cycle analysis this would be a significant factor and as noted elsewhere this can distort the validity of some methods of building assessment. Energy in use is of increasing importance as legislation begins to 'bite' but the costs of energy consumption figure are low in terms of occupier total costs. The findings of this project have reinforced the point of energy efficiency as being of low significance within the building to retain or develop decision-making process.

Likeability/loveability

These two are complimentary measures of a buildings functional and emotive performance. Likeability relates to how well the building is seen to meet the users and communities functional needs, it relates to matters of occupier satisfaction and the fitness for purpose and is essentially a quantitative assessment. Loveability refers to the emotional response to the building and is a qualitative assessment which can only be measured by reference to the responses by users and the community.

An occupier may love a building for its image

and character while bemoaning its functional qualities if for example all the lavatories are in the basement and for that reason may be said not to like the building. In a similar fashion the community may love a building for its appearance but not like using it due to its inaccessibility.

They are both related to social aspects of the building and will determine, in part at least, whether the building is considered worthy of being retained. It is in this area that conflicts between the requirements of internal and external stakeholders may arise. Where a building has statutory protection, the balance is effectively towards a recognition of its value in social terms, but even where it is not the issue should nevertheless be recognised and included within the dialogue.

Promoting sustainability within the existing building stock

In the UK the building stock has normally been replaced on a long-term cycle with no more than 2% of buildings replaced in any one year. It has been estimated that some 50% of current UK office floor area in use today dates from before 1964, with about half of this proportion dating from pre-1900.(5) The implications of this trend are that if TBL sustainability is to be achieved, part of the strategy must be the re-use of buildings where appropriate and their upgrading to achieve better social and environmental performance, a strong argument given the issue of embodied energy.

The decision as to whether to retain, alter or demolish a building is usually taken on economic grounds. Constraints on the decision-making process arise through the planning laws and, in some cases, the listing of the building. The latter however only applies where a building is of architectural or historic significance, not on the grounds of a potential 'fit' to sustainability criteria. Where a building is not listed, there is no requirement on the owner to take into account any notion of 'inter-generational equity', or indeed the views of community stakeholders; however, there is a growing requirement, as part of planning negotiations, to consider the needs of sustainability and Local Agenda 21. There is therefore a need to develop tools to enable these discussions to be well informed which is reflected in the assessment tool developed in Chapter 6.

Nevertheless the interests of sustainable development are not well served by the blanket retention of all stock. Given the requirement for buildings to work economically, socially and environmentally it is vital that a balanced approach is taken to the assessment of their future. Without such a balance there is a danger that towns and cities will become ossified and no longer work in the interests of those they serve.

Summary

The concept of sustainable development has been embraced internationally and has been simply defined in terms of the need to ensure inter-generational equity in all decision-making processes. This has been refined to refer to the concept of balancing decisions across the 'triple bottom line' (TBL) of economic viability, social well-being and environmental protection.

There is now a need, enshrined both in legislation and in social mores, to promote sustainable buildings. This raises the question of what constitutes a sustainable building. At first sight this might imply a 'green' building that is efficient in energy terms. However, the term embraces far more than this; it requires that the building operates successfully economically, environmentally and socially.

A new building can be designed to comply with TBL principles. The greater challenge arises in connection with decisions about existing stock. Should they be retained in their existing state, adapted for another use, or demolished? In the

past decisions have been driven by economic factors alone, except where a building is listed.

Moves towards greater sustainability require that a new approach be taken in respect of decisions concerning the future of existing buildings. It is important that the consequences of decisions to retain, with or without major modifications, or to demolish are taken with the aim of sustainable development in mind. The subsequent chapters develop this agenda in respect of the triple bottom line and a Building Sustainability Assessment Tool is proposed in the form of the assessment tool to inform the stakeholder dialogue.

Endnotes

1   While many local authorities have made significant strides in developing and implementing their Agenda 21 objectives, research (Morpeth, 2003) has shown that there is much variation between authorities.

2   Morse (2002) related the HDI (Human Development Index) to the ecological footprint, and states: 'Clearly, as one would expect, the HDI increases as the ecological footprint increases up to a point before levelling off.'

3   Examples of such developments are comparatively rare in the UK but Doxford Industrial Park is a zero energy building, while the new Wessex Water Headquarter building has recently received a major award for Energy Efficiency.

4   Sayce *et al.*, 2001 Business *Case for Sustainable Property*, commissioned by the Construction Confederation.

5   From the Bartlett School of Graduate Studies Non Domestic Building Stock Project, data as recorded on the Valuation Support application database for four bulk classes, England and Wales, 1994 (www.barlett.ucl.ac.uk/ndbs/valuationdata).

Chapter 2

Stakeholders Within Sustainable Development

Principal Messages:

- *Within conventional business operations the stakeholders in the decision-making process are easily defined. They are normally 'internal' to the organisation in that they have defined rights.*
- *The principle of sustainable development acknowledges the existence of 'external' stakeholders whose undefined, and often indefinable rights, must nevertheless be acknowledged.*
- *The role of government is to ensure, through legislation and the democratic process, that such external stakeholders are not ignored in corporate decision-making.*
- *If compliance with the principles of sustainable development is to be achieved the views of both internal and external stakeholders should be evaluated within the process.*
- *For individual buildings external stakeholders are not currently considered within the process except insofar as planning regulation dictates.*
- *The Building Sustainability Assessment Tool has been designed to ensure that external stakeholders' views can be incorporated within the decision-making process.*

The nature of a stakeholder

A stakeholder can be simply defined as any person or body, corporate or not, who has an interest in the building and its future. To this extent everyone is a stakeholder in the sustainable development debate and the Bruntland definition has been interpreted as a matter of intergenerational equity implying that future generations are stakeholders whose rights require defence in the same way as the present generation.

Under the concept of basic human rights, the rights of the individual can only be protected if it is recognised that protection must have an international dimension. For example, the purchase of imported goods may adversely affect the employability of indigenous labour, but an embargo on these goods may damage the economic future of the exporters. Similarly, in cross-generational terms, the exploitation of mineral extractions may produce either a short or long-term dividend depending upon the management process of the wealth so created. A balance needs to be struck between all stakeholders: the challenge is in recognising the requirements and assessing how best to achieve them.(1)

The concept of everyone being a stakeholder is attractive in principle but may be difficult in practice. This does not mean that the identification of stakeholders is not important (Vos, 2002) in business but that the identification of the appropriate stakeholders is even more important. Freeman (1984) provides a narrower definition in relation to corporate entities: he defines them as *'any group or individual who can affect or is affected by the achievement of the organisation's objectives'*. It follows that there are two aspects in the definition of a stakeholder:

- Those affected by the decision; and
- Those who affect the decision.

Sometimes the desires or needs of those affected

by decisions will conflict. In a democratic society the function of politics is to reconcile those differences in pragmatic ways to ensure minimal loss and optimal gain. This in itself is difficult but when the needs of future generations are included it becomes more so.

Stakeholder rights, responsibilities and risk

There are three main strands to the notion of a stakeholder:

- Rights;
- Responsibilities; and
- Risk participation.

It has been established that a stakeholder is someone (and this can include all forms of life (2)) who has **rights** that are consistent with the principles of sustainable development. These rights may or may not be protected and enforceable by legislation: supra-national, national or local. For example, the right to clean water is enshrined within UK law, but is not yet something that can be enforced within a global context although it is included within the Agenda 21 aspirations (www.un.org). In a corporate context employees and shareholders have readily defined rights, but the right to be regarded as a stakeholder may extend far beyond those legally definable confines.

In everyday activity the rights of people who at first sight appear to be external stakeholders have long been recognised. For example the law of negligence in the UK is founded on the principle that those without a contractual relationship may make a claim for an adverse affect suffered due to the negligent act or omission at the hands of a third party. The rise of the late twentieth century civil rights protest movement against many bodies corporate may be traced in part to a new claim of 'rights' exercised by those who feel that the democratic process offers insufficient protection (Heertz, 2001). These protests have been based largely on the claim that bodies corporate and governments have been too slow and/or too cynical in embracing sustainable development principles, especially in relation to social well-being and environmental degradation.

Wherever a right arises, there is a corresponding

responsibility. The responsibility lies with both the individual stakeholder and on those with the power, who will, by definition also be stakeholders. This raises the issue of relative power between stakeholders some of whom will have greater power, and responsibility than others as for example the Board of Directors of a company has significantly greater power than individual shareholder and so are normally deemed to have greater responsibility.

The rise of the notion of Corporate Social Responsibility (CSR), which has been argued by some to be no more than the formalisation of good business sense (3) is now enshrined in UK legislation affecting major institutional organisations. For example, the Trustees of occupational pension funds have obligations under the The Pensions Disclosure Regulations (2000) as to the extent to which social, environmental or ethical consider-ations are taken into account in their investment strategies and their policy (if any) in relation to the exercise of rights (including voting rights) attaching to investments (www.legislation.hmso.gov.uk).

This requires that consideration be given to the social and environmental dividend as well as to the economic and this in turn requires recognition of both internal and external stakeholders but increasingly there is a shift. The move towards CSR may have a regulatory element, but is being advocated as a means by which a company can retain competitive advantage; it is moving from the realms of best practice to normal practice (see for example Hopkins, 2003).

The third consequence of being a stakeholder lies in the distribution of **risk**. The concept of sustainability is essentially forward-looking in that all decision-making today will affect the lives and experiences of those who follow. The quality of decision-making can only be evaluated with the passage of time: for example, the decision to demolish a building is irreversible and once the building has gone, perhaps because it was not deemed important in cultural terms and was not at the time economically viable, it cannot be replaced. In retrospect, the demolition of Victorian cottages and their replacement by high-rise blocks has proved a socially damaging decision. Similarly, during the post World War II period, planning consent was given for many roadside restaurant developments in rural areas without an agricultural

Abandoned road side buildings, Hindhead, Surrey This abandoned restaurant represents unsustainable development. As transport and social patterns have changed so have the needs for roadside development which is often suffering competition from competing schemes in town centres. This can be seen clearly from these derelict buildings on the A3 south of Hindhead, Surrey.

restoration condition. As the routes they served have systematically been by-passed, many have become uneconomic and fallen into disuse, resulting in eyesores and wasteland.

Decision-making involves risk. Under any conventional business model, risks will be factored in and priced, and where appropriate, depending on negotiating strength, will be shared between the parties.

In the case of sustainable development many of the social and environmental risks are borne by those who cannot be actively involved in the decision-making process, as they are outside it. If sustainability principles are to be adopted, the decision-making process must be reviewed to ensure that those internal to the process recognise this situation and respond by evaluating the risks and containing them rather than by simply passing them on.

The process of incorporating risk within the decision-making process can be developed diagrammatically:

Figure 2.1 The TRAP of risk

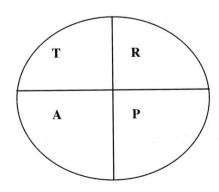

Legend:

T – Take on the risk
R – Reject the risk
A – Ameliorate the risk
P – Pass on the risk

The TRAP diagram demonstrates that where risk is identified there are only four possible responses to it. First (T) it can be taken on as an inevitable consequence of the action. It can be argued that in many ways this has been society's individual and collective response to environmental matters. The risks in terms of environmental degradation associated with wealth-creation were neither factored in nor priced. They were implicitly accepted. Only in the last thirty years, with the rise of the environmental lobby and the warning cries of commentators such as Schumacher (1973) and Lovelock (1979), has the notion of world survival been questioned.

Within an individual project, the option of rejecting the risk (R) is normally open, albeit all alternative courses of action may bear some risk. If a sustainability perspective is taken, while internal stakeholders may be able to reject risk, external stakeholders cannot as they are not in a position of control. Additionally, as no mechanism exists for full 'future-proofing', the risk cannot be rejected. It exists and someone must bear the consequences. The difficulty is in who controls the risk and who pays the price of any problems that arise.

In reality, most sustainable development is concerned with ameliorating (A) or lessening the risks by developing a series of positive actions to counter-balance them. For example, environmental and social legislation and economic fiscal measures have been imposed on individuals, businesses and properties to limit future degradation and protect the needs of external stakeholders, including those of future generations. In building terms the most obvious example of this is in listed buildings where a judgement is made that there is a risk that the cultural and heritage value will be lost to both present and future generations and that this must be reduced by giving statutory protection.

Lastly, risk may be passed on (P) in part or in full, as for example under an insurance policy. Such a scenario may be appropriate where risks can be adequately evaluated and financial or other equitable recompense made. Without protective action, it is often possible to pass on risk to external stakeholders at no cost to the internal stakeholders.

From the above analysis it can be seen that the decision-maker's view of risk management will be focused entirely on the effects of risk to those who are internal to the process and within these terms it will be built into the financial appraisal process.

Listed buildings and cultural heritage: Harley Street London
Famous as the home for medical practitioners the original residential buildings have been adapted successfully due to the particular occupational requirements of medical practitioners. They are able to make sensible use of small cellular spaces while the major rooms provide reception areas. The impact of new legislation such as access for the disabled however presents fresh challenges to their use for this purpose.

The needs of those who may be affected by decisions are not incorporated, unless they can exercise a powerful influence (for example citizen action) to the extent that legislation or political pressure can affect behaviour. The alternative approach is one of persuasion – that by taking on the requirements of the TBL, including the external view, the risks to the internal stakeholders are actually reduced. This argument known as 'beyond compliance' is taking hold as more businesses espouse the stance that 'sustainability pays'. (See for example The Brookings Institute, 2002; Hopkins, 2003; Margolis and Walsh, 2001.)

If an 'all stakeholder' perspective is adopted, the possibility of passing on risk becomes unacceptable unless it has been fully priced within some form of full cost accounting, that builds on both internal and external factors.(4) From the above, it is apparent that to comply with TBL principles of sustainability, the views and needs of external stakeholders should be included or they will bear risk without any fair recompense. The real difficulty remains in identifying the risks that are implied in any course of action.(5)

Stakeholders in property and construction

Within the built environment, the stakeholder community is universal. Buildings and the places they create, provide the backdrop to most human activity and this has economic social and environmental dimensions. They provide the means for both wealth creation (e.g. factories and offices properties) and wealth consumption (e.g. leisure and retail premises) and thus they have economic influences on external stakeholders. Their design, visual impact and accessibility are matters of importance to all who use them or even pass by. They are capable of evoking both practical and emotional responses and they therefore have social implications.

For example the urban grain produced by a collection of aesthetically pleasing buildings can evoke a feeling of well-being which in turn can promote tourism with its economic and environmental consequences, both positive and negative. Buildings that individually or collectively produce landscapes that are dull or depressing have been connected with social ills. (See for example, Coleman, 1985; Newman, 1972; Cooper and Sarkissian, 1986; Kaplan and Kaplan, 1982.) They

also have other external impacts: as producers of almost half the carbon emissions and as major users of finite physical resources, their construction and use have environmental consequences for both internal and external stakeholders.

Identifying the stakeholders

In order to promote sustainability within the existing building stock the identity of the major stakeholder groups must be established. At first sight this is simple: the building owner and occupier are internal stakeholders; all others are external. However, such an interpretation is incomplete.

Occupiers and owners may have a legal and financial stake in a building but they are not necessarily the only people with a financial interest. Many commercial buildings are financed by loan finance which extends the possible internal remit to the financiers. Consultant teams involved with building construction and the subsequent maintenance and management of a building also have a direct interest and could be regarded as internal stakeholders.

The external stakeholder group includes all those with no direct legal, equitable or financial interest in the building, but who are nevertheless affected by decisions about it. These include not just the populace but those users of a building such as shoppers who are affected by, but unable to affect, decisions. For most buildings the extent of their influence will be small but for landmark buildings, the external stakeholders take on a far wider significance.

More problematic is the determination of the status of those who work for building occupiers, for example sales assistants and office employees. They may have no direct legal or financial stake in the building, but in so far as they have a financial (if not legal) interest in the occupier, they are taken to be internal stakeholders. Within a shopping precinct, shoppers would normally be taken to be external stakeholders, since while they undoubtedly contribute financially to the economic success or otherwise of the property, they have no direct powers to influence decisions.

The position of local authorities and other public bodies is even more ambiguous. In many instances they are landowners and even where they are not they have a pecuniary interest in terms of rate revenue etc. in the prosperity or otherwise of the areas for which they have responsibility. As well as planning authorities they are representatives of the external stakeholder community.

As with the generic issues relating to stake-holding, building developers, owners and occupiers have rights and responsibilities and they will adopt attitudes to risk. In terms of the latter, the preference of investing owners has been towards transference of risk to occupiers through devices such as full repairing leases. Such arrangements have not led to constructive dialogue even between groups of internal stakeholders but work by the Sustainable Construction Task Group (2002) has demonstrated that building owners and developers who seek an internal economic perspective only are likely to be incurring more risk than those who adopt TBL principles.

The identification of external stakeholders and their views formed an important part of the *Buildings: a new life* project and the clashes in their interests is examined in Appendix A. For example, to the planners, matters such as amenities and public transport were high on the list of items that affected their views on a building's life while to occupiers and owners car parking was of greater importance!

The Building Sustainability Assessment Tool

The Building Sustainability Assessment Tool detailed in Chapter 6 is designed to ensure that the views of both internal and external stakeholders are recognised. For example, the investing building owner will frequently take a primarily short-term economic view while the planners need to take a long-term perspective recognising external stakeholder needs. This goes to the heart of the debate and ensures that a true dialogue may be undertaken which respects the views of others and seeks to arrive at a balanced assessment.

Summary

For truly sustainable development it is clear that decisions should be taken that recognise the presence of both internal and external stakeholders.

It is recognised that all stakeholders have rights, whether or not they are enshrined in legislation.

The notion of a stakeholder is difficult to define: it implies not only rights but also responsibilities and some form of risk acceptance. While the first two can be dealt with within the legislative frameworks, risk identification and management is more difficult. Attitudes to risk are frequently developed from the point of view of an internal decision making stake-holder point of view. To meet the sustainability criteria this concept must be extended to include an understanding of how risk affects those external to the decision-making process.

A stakeholder may be defined as a person or organisation who has a financial or legal interest in a building. The decision-making process involved in determining the future life of a building should take into account the needs of both internal and external stakeholders. The Building Sustainability Assessment Tool has been developed to enable a constructive dialogue to take place that accepts the actual and potential conflicts that inevitably exist between the interests of internal and external parties.

Endnotes

1   For a debate of such issues and the need to achieve balance see Naomi Klein's book *No Logo* (2001) in which she tracks in much detail some of the consequences in the third world of first world marketing imperatives.

2   Sylvan and Bennett 1994 Comparison of shallow, intermediate and deep environmentalism of which the last argues that human beings are not of greater value than other things in the natural world.

3   There is much debate, which lies outside the scope of this work, into what constitutes real corporate social responsibility. Welford (2000) in his book *Corporate Environmental Management* argues that organisations can adopt different levels of engagement with sustainable development, from a first (superficial) level of technological engagement to higher levels that culminate in real change to 'core values' and principles.

4   For a discussion of full cost accounting (FCA) principles and how they have been developed by one organisation see Bebbington *et al.*, (2001). This details a model (the Sustainability Assessment Method) produced by BP to enable them to analyse specific project performance in terms of the TBL.

5   The issue of what risks to identify is very difficult. For example, at a global level the Kyoto Protocol called on nation states to take action against the risks of climate change. However, by signing up to (and hence accepting the risk) arguably a country was exposing itself to the risk of greater burden on the economy.

Chapter 3

Economic Sustainability of Buildings

Principal Messages:

- *There is no single definition of economic sustainability: it depends on the prevailing economic system.*
- *Current prevailing economic concepts acknowledge but do not make full allowance for external costs and benefits (i.e. those relating to external stakeholders).*
- *There are moves to connect corporate economic sustainability with the adoption of TBL principles.*
- *Economic success and economic sustainability are not synonymous.*
- *The key features of a building lie in its ability to remain efficient and economic in the hands of both occupier and owner.*
- *If economic viability is not achieved and there is a lack of occupational demand; however socially or environmentally sustainable the building, it is at risk of failure.*

Economic sustainability: a definition

Definitions of economic sustainability abound. Hutton (2001) relates it to a concept of 'progressive profitability' by which he means that the pursuit of simple profit is not enough. Zadek and Tuppen (2000) suggest that there must be a dividend in terms of environmental and social outcomes. At its simplest it can be defined as that economic activity which continues in the short and long term to the extent that the revenue or over all return generated exceeds the cost of its creation.

Such a simple definition is attractive but also misleading. What is meant by 'all return' and what are all the costs? Do they extend to those incurred by people not directly related to the investment proposition? In short should external stakeholders be included in developing calculations of the economic return?

Doane and MacGillivray (2001: section 0.3) argue that *'economic sustainability is the most elusive component of the triple bottom line approach'*. The reasons for this are not hard to

discover. The basic assumption is that, within the corporate world at least, the profit motivation will be the driving force behind strategy and actions. It is not a driver that is easily disturbed. Hence, the proponents of the sustainability agenda have concentrated on developing knowledge and awareness of environmental and social concerns and sought to make a connection between the adoption of enlightened environmental policies, good governance and economic success. Therefore it has been, and can be, argued that economic sustainability is best assured by compliance with the other two heads of the triple bottom line.

Measuring economic sustainability: from global to organisational measurement

Starting with the global perspective it is clear that definitions of economic sustainability mean different things to different groups of people – depending on their relationship with the organisation under consideration. Economic sustainability is usually considered in terms of gross domestic product

(GDP), real incomes and a range of other indicators, including employment. The World Bank tracks a range of indicators to measure success including economic prosperity measured in GDP terms, economic growth rates, debt and its ability to be managed and savings and investment (www.worldbank.org).

The Bruntland Report (OECD, 1987) called for acceleration in the rate of economic growth, tempered with due environmental consideration, as the main mechanism to move towards economic sustainability (as opposed to success). By this it meant that short-run economic success is not necessarily sustainable, nor are economic returns that are won only at the expense of adverse environmental impacts or negative social consequences.

Since that time moves have been made towards the development of a measurement index, but this remains contentious and incomplete (see for

example Morse, 2001). Further, the connectivity between increases in GDP, as conventionally measured, and sustainability, is being questioned.

The challenge to current measures of economic analysis with their inherent assumptions regarding economic growth has been made by some economists over many years. (See for example Galbraith, 1958, Mishan, 1967 and 1972). More recently, others have taken up the argument (Forum for the Future, 1996; Von Weizsacker *et al.*, 1997; Hawken *et al.*, 1999). Economic *success*, it is argued, may be an essential component of economic *sustainability*, but the two are not synonymous.

While the global perspective is of major importance the need for sustainability comes home to the community though local issues and the Rio Summit in 1992 promoted, as Agenda 21, the development of local sustainability initiatives (www.un.org). The agreement on Agenda 21,

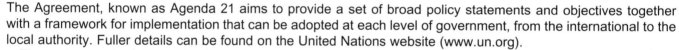

Box 3.1 Local Agenda 21

The Agreement, known as Agenda 21 aims to provide a set of broad policy statements and objectives together with a framework for implementation that can be adopted at each level of government, from the international to the local authority. Fuller details can be found on the United Nations website (www.un.org).

The main principles of the Agenda are to:
- Co-operate in accelerating sustainable development in developing countries together with related domestic development.
- Combat poverty.
- Change patterns of consumption.
- Better understand and respond to the interaction between demographics dynamics and sustainability.
- Protect and promote public health conditions.
- Promote sustainable human settlement developments.
- Integrate environmental and development matters within policy decision-making.
- Protect the atmosphere.
- Integrate approaches to planning and managing land resources.
- Combat deforestation.
- Manage fragile eco-systems by limiting deforestation and drought.
- Promote sustainable mountain development.
- Promote sustainable agriculture and rural development.
- Conserve bio-diversity.
- Promote environmentally sound biotechnology.
- Protect the oceans and seas and coastal zones.
- Protect the quality and supply of freshwater.
- Promote environmentally sound management of toxic chemicals.
- Promote environmentally sound management of hazardous waste.
- Promote environmentally sound management of solid waste and sewage.
- Promote safe and environmentally sound management of radioactive waste.

signed by some 178 nations in 1992 called for action to promote both social and economic development that conserves and manages the environment. The Agenda was confirmed as part of the Johannesburg Summit negotiations in 2001.

The UK government has taken this up and local authorities are encouraged to develop 'Quality of Life Indicators'.(1) Many have done so, although coverage is estimated to be less than 50% (Higginson *et al.*, 2003).

Although the Audit Commission (2002) has developed a template, each local authority is free to develop their own indicators, but all must cover the triple bottom line. For example, London First Sustainability Unit has produced a 'Triple Bottom Line' Index for London (London First, 2001) with the aim of tracking whether or not London is becoming a more or less sustainable city. Their index for economic sustainability is based on the following criteria:

- *Gross Domestic Product*. This measures the overall size of London's economy.
- *Investment*. For this, Office of National Statistics figures are used to measure private sector investment. (But there is an on-going debate as to whether this includes fixed tangible investment and/or soft 'in-tangible' investment, such as education which is so important in a knowledge-based economy.)
- *Sectoral Performance*. This measures environmental performance using the results of an annual survey of businesses. It is therefore a selective sample indicator.
- *London plc*. Using the Dow Jones Sustainability Index criteria this seeks to measure overall performance of the city. Again it is a highly selective indicator.
- *New Firm Formation*. Based on DTI (Department of Trade and Industry) data this measures entrepreneurial activity.

This list is rather different from that proposed by some other authorities, which may be more extensive in terms of number, but many of which exclude some of the key investment criteria deemed appropriate for London by Sustainability First.

It is of note that, even at the level of the city, there is difficulty in arriving at an appropriate range of indicators for which data is available. While London First have been able to show the relative performance between one year and the next of economic, environmental and social indicators, the major debate and analysis relates to how one set of indicators relates to the other two sets.

Additionally, the factors listed above still focus very much on the internal stakeholder perspective. For example, the measure of GDP does not build within it allowance for social costs. It is not a fully costed accounting indicator.

None the less, as the desire to move towards TBL principles takes increasing hold, so the introduction of indicator sets will become more common and, in turn, more influential in terms of shaping policy, including planning land use policy. In this regard, the Audit Commission (www.audit-commission.gov.uk) tracks the progress of local authorities towards fulfilment of these objectives via their comprehensive performance assessment. They have also published a template for Quality of Life Indicators (see Box 3.2).

It is therefore vital that all those involved with property decision making in terms of building life should be aware of the Quality of Life Indicators and sustainability policy of the local authority in whose area the property is located.

Economic sustainability at the organisational level

The measurement of economic success of an individual organisation will normally be viewed in relation to standard accounting precepts. It is normally a matter of liquidity, profitability and balance sheet reserves. However, success, as measured in the short-term, does not constitute sustainability, which is essentially a long-term concept.

Douane and MacGillivray (2001:0.3) conclude that '*there are few tried, tested, acceptable, available and affordable management tools and systems*' that can be used to measure economic *sustainability*. To them this has to extend beyond the simple balance sheet to include issues such as:

- What constitutes appropriate longevity?
- How do you measure intellectual capital?
- What steps must be taken in the interests of prudent risk management?

Box 3.2 Quality of Life indicators

Economic

QoL 1   Proportion of people of working age in employment

QoL 2   Proportion of people claiming unemployment benefit who have been out of work for more than a year

QoL 3   Proportion of young people (18-24 year olds) in full-time education or employment

QoL 4   Percentage increase or decrease in the total number of VAT registered businesses in the area

QoL 5   Percentage increase or decrease in the number of local jobs

Social

QoL 6   Proportion of the population who live in wards that rank within the most deprived 10 per cent and/or 25 per cent of wards in the country

QoL 7   Percentage of population of working age who are claiming key benefits

QoL 8   Proportion of children under 16 who live in low income households

QoL 9   (a)   Proportion of 19 year olds with Level 2 qualifications (that is 5 GCSEs A*–C or NVQ equivalent)
         (b)   Percentage of 15 year old pupils in schools maintained by the local authority achieving 5 or more GCSEs at grades A*–C or equivalent

QoL 10   Death rate by cause (standardised mortality rate per 100,000 population in the following categories):
- cancer in under 75s
- circulatory diseases in under 75s
- suicide and undetermined injury – all ages
- all accidents – all ages

QoL 11   Infant mortality (number of deaths of infants under a year old and number of stillbirths – per 1,000 live births)

QoL 12   Rate of conceptions among girls aged less than 18 years

QoL 13   Affordable housing (house price/earnings affordability ratio)

QoL 14   Number of unfit homes per 1,000 dwellings

QoL 15   (a)   Percentage of residents surveyed who feel 'fairly safe' or 'very safe' after dark while outside in the local authority area
         (b)   Percentage of residents surveyed who feel 'fairly safe' or 'very safe' during the day while outside in the local authority area

QoL 16   Crimes committed:
- domestic burglaries (per 1,000 households)
- violent offences (per 1,000 population)
- vehicle crimes (per 1,000 population)

QoL 17   Percentage of residents surveyed who are concerned about different types of noise in their area

QoL 18   Percentage of residents surveyed who are satisfied with their local area as a place to live

QoL 19   Percentage of residents surveyed who consider that their local area is getting worse

QoL 20   Number of childcare places per 1,000 population aged 0–5 not in early education

QoL 21   Facilities for young people indicator(s) - under development, will be added in the future

QoL 22   (a)   Percentage of residents surveyed finding it easy to access key local services
         (b)   Actual distance to key local services

Social – community involvement

QoL 23   Percentage of adults surveyed who feel they can influence decisions affecting their local area

QoL 24   Percentage of voluntary/community organisations functioning in a specified locality per 1000 residents that performed well in the past year

QoL 25   Percentage of people surveyed who feel that their local area is a place where people from different backgrounds and communities can live together harmoniously

QoL 26   (a)   Percentage of people surveyed who have carried out any of a specified list of actions, unpaid, for someone who is not a relative in the past 12 months
         (b)   Percentage of people surveyed who have received any of a specified list of actions, unpaid, by someone who is not a relative in the past 12 months

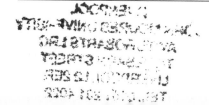

Box 3.2 Quality of Life indicators (continued)

Environmental

QoL 27 Air pollution

    (a)   Number of days per year when air pollution is 'moderate' or 'higher' for PM10

    (b)   Annual average nitrogen dioxide concentration

    (c)   For rural sites, number of days per year when air pollution is 'moderate' or 'higher' for ozone

QoL 28 Carbon dioxide emissions by sector (tonnes per year) and per capita emissions (tonnes)

QoL 29 Percentage of main rivers and canals rated as 'good' or 'fair' quality

QoL 30 Household energy use (gas and electricity) per household

QoL 31 Water leakage rate from main and customer pipes

QoL 32 Percentage of the total tonnage of household waste that has been:

- recycled
- composted
- used to recover heat, power and other energy sources
- landfilled

QoL 33 (a)   Proportion of land stock that is derelict

       (b)   Percentage of new housing development on previously developed land

QoL 34 Percentage of highways that are either of a 'high' or 'acceptable' standard of cleanliness

QoL 35 Annual average traffic flow per 1000 km of principal roads

QoL 36 Percentage of residents surveyed who used different modes of transport, their reasons for, and distance of, travel

QoL 37 Percentage of children travelling to (a) primary school, and (b) secondary school by different modes

QoL 38 The area of land designated as a Site of Special Scientific Interest (SSSI) and that is in 'favourable condition'

- number and hectares of land designated as a SSSI in a local authority area
- percentage of assessed area in favourable and unfavourable recovering condition, within SSSIs
- area of Local Nature Reserve per 1000 population (ha)
- local species count, for example wild birds, amphibians, water voles and so on

Source: Audit Commission (2002). *Using Quality of Life Indicators, Appendix A*

The work of Bebbington *et al.* (2001) with BP promotes a Sustainability Assessment Method to take full account of costs and benefits but this relates to the individual *project* (not organisational) level.

At the level of the business organisation or the town, economic sustainability is an important, but as yet unresolved, issue. Interest is being further fuelled, at the corporate level by the observed relationship between adoption of TBL principles and financial success, as measured by stock market performance.

The introduction of the Dow Jones Sustainability Index in 1995 provided an opportunity for comparison to be made between those companies whose adherence to ethical and environmental polices gave them access to the index and those companies who didn't. The results demonstrated higher levels of performance by the sustainability index over the all company index. This has proved a further stimulus. The more recent introduction (2001) of the FTSE4Good index has proved to be a similarly important tool as a driver to the corporate world to review their practices to ensure inclusion criteria are met.

Accommodating external stakeholders within a framework for economic sustainability

The analysis above points to a view of economic sustainability that is still inward focused, although the views of the external stakeholders are becoming of increasing importance. It is well recognised within economic theory that all 'private' economic decisions have external consequences or 'externalities'. In other words, every action has a social consequence, which goes beyond the immediate economic considerations of the private decision maker and affects external stakeholders. For example, the private use of a building creates CO_2 emissions and may cause air pollution, while the travel to it can lead to traffic congestion. As was argued in Chapter 2, in sustainability terms everyone is a stakeholder – even those belonging to subsequent generations.

Economists have considered external costs by many means, most notably Social Cost–Benefit Analysis. This works on the principle of shadow price substitution – namely that money is an inadequate compensation mechanism. However, this is not always an equitable or appropriate solution. At the simplest level the winning of non-renewable resources, such as coal, may provide benefits to the current generation, but it is a cost to those who come afterwards. In some cases, the external effects are felt immediately. For example, the development of a new airport brings high cost in terms of pollution and congestion to those living close by as well as environmental degradation and possible loss in terms of bio-diversity. While these factors have long been built into the planning system (2) for large-scale developments, currently by way of Environmental Impact Assessments, society does not factor in all externalities, especially at the level of small-scale projects.

It can be argued that, if the social cost is the loss of say an energy source such as coal, that may be replaceable by energy from renewable resources such as wind or solar power. If the resource that is being used up becomes in very short supply, not only will the pricing mechanism slow demand, but it will simultaneously stimulate the development of alternatives. Such is the rather optimistic view of some commentators (for example, Hawken *et al.*, 1999 track many examples of technology advance to overcome resource depletion).

For some goods such as species loss, clean air and water, there is no possible substitution. In these cases, the pricing model cannot stimulate the creation of alternative goods and the cost must fall on the external stakeholders. At its most radical, some commentators call for a total change in patterns of consumption in order to regain a

scientific harmony with the planet, in accordance with the theory of Gaia (Lovelock, 1979, Bunyard, 1996).

Acknowledgement of the rights of external stakeholders will determine approaches to economic systems management. At one extreme, a command economy, such as communism, places the onus on government for making decisions about resource allocation; at the other a fully deregulated market economy relies on the 'guiding hand' principle first developed by Adam Smith to ensure self-regulation.

In practice, as the sustainability agenda has gained momentum the UK government, partly in response to EU and world objectives (e.g. the Kyoto Protocol), has increasingly operated both a 'carrot and stick' approach through legal and fiscal measures to ensure that a wider stakeholder perspective is adopted. This in turn has led to many commentators advocating the benefits of a 'beyond compliance' approach being good for business – the 'sustainability pays' argument.

Economic sustainability for buildings – wealth creating versus wealth consuming buildings

Any discussion of buildings and economic sustainability needs to be preceded with a brief understanding of how buildings relate to the creation and consumption of wealth. Very broadly, buildings can be categorised into wealth creating buildings and wealth spending buildings (see Box 3.3).

It is acknowledged that the classification is simplistic. For example, it could be argued that retail buildings are both wealth creating and wealth consuming buildings. The broad categorisation is open to debate but it does provide a starting point from which to consider economic sustainability.

The highest productivity (high rental values often imply high productivity) is generally seen in new buildings, such as office developments like Broadgate in the City of London, Canary Wharf or Stockley Park near Heathrow. This is a combination of the function of location (i.e. proximity to markets), and the extent to which the building form and design is compliant with the requirements of the user. These illustrate a general point but there are many exceptions as efficient buildings are built in

---

Box 3.3 Wealth-creating versus wealth-consuming buildings

Wealth-creating buildings
Wealth-creating buildings mainly meet the core human hierarchy of needs relating to: air, water, food, shelter and safety.
   They include:

- Agricultural Buildings
- Industrial Manufacturing Buildings
- Industrial Distribution Buildings
- Office Buildings

Wealth-consuming buildings
Wealth-consuming buildings relate to a higher hierarchy of needs in relation to: social needs, love, attention, personal growth, emotional pleasures and intellectual exploration. Some examples are:

- Government Office Buildings
- Retail High Street Locations
- Retail Shopping Centres
- Retail Warehouses
- Retail Food Stores
- Retail Factory Outlets
- Tourist Retail Outlets
- Leisure and Entertainment Buildings (theatres, nightclubs)
- Museums/Art Galleries/Sports Venues
- Places of Worship/Churches/Villages Halls
- Health/Hospitals
- Education/Schools and Universities
- Military Buildings
- Transport Facilities
- Housing/Residential Buildings
- Listed Buildings range from the Post Office Tower to Tank Traps ... etc.

---

areas of low value and periods of high economic activity associated with the development of both wealth-creating and wealth-spending buildings may change the perceived high value areas, at least for the duration of this activity.

The most economically productive industrial buildings also tend to be new, such as the Honda car facility at Swindon or the Nissan car facility in Sunderland while Ham Halls and Magna Park in the Midlands are examples of new efficient industrial distribution buildings. As with offices, the building's physical characteristics and configuration are related closely to economic viability.

It should be noted here that while many efficient large production processes tend to take place in modern buildings, efficient plant can be installed in older buildings where with low rent and capital cost

already written off, economic sustainability can be achieved even though the building may be spatially inefficient and lacking environmentally acceptable standards.

With time a wealth-creating building becomes less fit for its purpose and its value to the occupier will decline. Usually this will manifest itself in lower rental growth, with a consequential decline in value for the investor. Depreciation has been defined as '*a loss in the real existing use value of property*' (Baum, 1994: 545), or more graphically by Bowie as '*the inevitable march to the scrapheap*' (Bowie, 1982: 405).

Physical deterioration and obsolescence are the major causes of lower values. Although a building constructed from poor quality materials or to a poor design may lose value, obsolescence is a more

Broadgate, City of London
Wealth-creating buildings
created on the site of a
former railway goods yard.
This major development met
not only economic but also
social objectives with the
incorporation of a focal
meeting and leisure activity
in the form of the multi-
purpose skating area over-
looked by bars and
restaurants

common reason for depreciation in economic
viability. Researchers have categorised obsolescence as aesthetic, functional, legal and social
(Salway, 1986). The RICS (2003) also consider the
question of depreciation in the context of
specialised buildings. In *Rubbish Theory* Thompson
describes the role of what he terms the 'taste
makers' in reversing depreciation and cites case
studies in the Islington housing market during the
second half of the 20th century to support his
argument. Here the interests of the internal and
external stakeholders have combined to create an
economic and environmentally sustainable context
although the increase in property values challenged
the social sustainability of a balanced community
(Thompson, 1979).

The following points are identified from a study
of the literature as contributing to depreciation:

- Physical deterioration: the finishes or/and
  structure require significant expenditure;
- Economic or environmental obsolescence: the
  building suffers a decline in value from
  changing external economic factors either in
  the locality of the wider economy;
- Functional obsolescence: the building is no
  longer fit for its purpose sometimes because of
  technological change;

- Aesthetic obsolescence: the building no longer
  meets the style or fashion of the period and
  cannot give the occupier the desired 'status';
- Legal obsolescence: changes in legislation
  render the building less unusable or in need of
  expenditure (e.g. building regulation changes)
  or less valuable (e.g. changes to tenant
  protection legislation);
- Social obsolescence: the building is no longer
  appropriately located.

Baum goes on to argue that flexibility and
configuration are key considerations in providing
protection against falling value (Baum, 1994). In
the *Buildings: a new life* project it was found that
building adaptability was a key factor with
configuration being of less importance.

In that study the focus was on existing
commercial buildings. The key to combating
depreciation rests in many cases on whether they
are wealth-creating or wealth-consuming
buildings. If the former, the question of functional
obsolescence may be a key consideration as with
a factory or office, where a prime criterion is that
the most effective working practices can be
adopted.

Wealth-consuming buildings tend to be less
prone to functional obsolescence and image or

The Light, Leeds
A major multi-level city centre mixed use development utilising listed buildings to provide a four star hotel and catering with an L-shaped arcade and a block of new building housing a multiplex, health club and at basement level a 600 space car park. This leisure destination provides purpose-built accommodation for the larger units which benefit from the atmosphere created by the historic structures.

Architects: DLG Architects

nostalgic associations can be of greater significance. For example, with a use such as a restaurant, the needs of the occupier are more easily accommodated in a range of structures and a variety of configurations. Retailing, as an activity, is normally more dependent on location than physical factors, provided that the building can comply with legislation, although there are some retailers such as food stores where the constraints of gondola layout and aisle widths will be as important as for an industrial production line.

Leisure uses in particular may be particularly suited to the 'quirky' and the old and some even accentuate age and where a unique character may add to the economic value. This does not hold good for all leisure buildings, the spatial requirements of

Docklands warehousing, London
These buildings which were the subject of one of the case studies illustrate the change in value as they move from redundant wealth creating buildings to a new use as wealth-consuming uses.

multiplex cinemas and bowling alleys can rarely be accommodated in historic buildings. Economic and functional obsolescence may have many different aspects but the one essential feature is the capability to adapt with time to meet new requirements, Brand (1997).

Economic viability of buildings

As discussed above a building's form and construction has long-term implications even with regard to its demolition and the possible reuse of its elements. Most buildings, with adequate maintenance, are capable of survival over considerable periods even when designed like the post war pre-fab for a finite life-span.(3) The design life of a building is increasingly governed by life-cycle costing considerations but despite the existence of a specific life expectation in practice economic sustainability will normally outweigh other considerations in determining its life span.

However environmentally or socially sustainable and important a building may be, if it does not work economically it will be downgraded in value, possibly change use and may fall into disrepair and disuse unless it is given protection, as a listed

building.(4) Even then its future is not necessarily assured, as many listed buildings fail (English Heritage, 2001, Scanlon *et al.*, 1994). Such failure is usually associated with a lack of future economic use and of available funds for maintenance. Indeed there is an argument that listing is a re-action taken precisely because there is a conflict across the triple bottom line.

There will also be situations where a building survives simply because the site value is too low to render redevelopment viable and this in turn can alter over time due to a range of external factors including public investment or the effects of changing technological demands.(5) There have been a number of cases where low value wealth creating buildings such as dockside warehousing have been given a new lease of life by a change in the nature of the location one of wealth spending leisure activities, taking positive advantage of the environmental qualities of the location.

As the UK economy has changed from one based initially on agriculture, through an industrial based era to what is often described as a service model it has now developed into an 'experience' economy where added value is achieved through the quality of the experience of making the

---

Box 3.4: Example of public finance stimulated development: the case of Canary Wharf

The creation of Enterprise Zones in the 1980s in the UK resulted in a number of major new urban projects, the flagship of which was the Canary Wharf development in London's Docklands. However, by the early 1990s, the Olympia and York's 4.4-million sq ft office development had become spectacularly bankrupt. This was due, not only to the world recession (resulting from the public expenditure excesses of the President Reagan 1980s and the deregulation of the UK economy) but also to lack of public expenditure on transport facilities.

Eventually more than £4 billion was spent by taxpayers (according to PA International and Cambridge University report and their analysis of the public benefit to this Enterprise Zone), in the form of:

- A new Jubilee Line Underground railway;
- A new Docklands Light Railway, a new road network in Popular in East London;
- Taxation allowances on expenditure within the zone and expenditure in the form of London Docklands Development Corporations; and
- Relief from Uniform Business Rates.

These costs resulted in the Canary Wharf scheme eventually becoming profitable privately. Economic sustainability at Canary Wharf, and Canary Wharf plc appearing in the FTSE 100 listing, has only been achieved by a mixture of both public and private investment.

---

purchase or utilising the service (Pine and Gilmore, 1999). Some buildings have shown greater flexibility than others have in accommodating these new ways of working.

This theme is taken up by Brand (1997) who demonstrates that a building must adapt over time in order to succeed and to contribute to the urban scene. Building flexibility can provide not only economic return to internal stakeholders but also a social benefit to external stakeholders. These factors are explored further by Kincaid (2001) in his useful analysis of factors that determine building adaptation.

Because of the internal stakeholders ability, usually reflected in matters such as the terms of their lease, to transfer their interest to another location, for them the prime economic consideration will normally be short-term. For the community however, it is the long-term contribution that the building can make to its environment and the local economy that is more important. There will often be a conflict between these stakeholder groups when short-term considerations render the building uneconomic to its occupiers and owners, yet it is regarded as adding value to an area where this is measured in terms other than strictly financial.

It is not surprising therefore that, despite the prevalence of market pressures, the process and fiscal policy framework is built on legislation aimed at social enhancement and environmental protection. It is in this situation, where a building has importance to an area and may in the future be capable of offering private sector viability, that there is a potential case for 'gap' funding by the external stakeholders.

As the example in Box 3.4 illustrates, to be economically sustainable new construction in deprived or changing locations must rely upon a mixture of public and private finance. The debate continues on the ways in which this should be achieved: while most would agree that the regeneration of rundown areas does require 'pump-priming' through the public purse, others consider that appropriate fiscal measures based on land taxation may be preferable to stimulate redevelopment and refurbishment interest by providing fiscal incentives and penalties (Riley, 2001).

If it is accepted that regeneration and protection of historic environments and buildings requires public money, then choices must be made. Which buildings are best preserved or conserved? Is listing, which focuses solely on architectural and historic importance the only appropriate mechanism for identification? John Allan writing a summary chapter for English Heritage's *Preserving Post-War Heritage* papers called for a wider agenda than that of 'straight' conservation to be

Canary Wharf, London

Canary Wharf has re-emerged as a lively commercial and residential location after tortuous early years and problems over the provision of the transport infrastructure. It has taken a decade for the social transformation to emerge following the physical regeneration.

brought to bear. He suggested that the application of modern conservation need to go beyond the '*picket fence of statutory listing*' and '*move away from revering buildings as vessels of culture towards re-valuing buildings as a social resource*' (Macdonald, 2001). This argues that the choice is essentially one in which the whole triple bottom line approach should be adopted.

It is this assumption on which the Building Sustainability Assessment Tool (Chapter 6) has been developed. If the tool reveals that a building can effectively contribute across the TBL from the external stakeholder perspective, but that it is vulnerable in conventional (internal) short-term economic terms, there might be a case for external (public) financial support – whether or not it is listed. If the tool reveals that it has little value to external stakeholders, then the views of internal stakeholders will prevail and these, as argued above, will tend to be dominated by matters of economic viability.

Before detailing the economic sustainability factors shown by *Buildings: a new life* research to affect decisions surrounding retention or demolition, the factors driving the economic value of buildings are briefly outlined from the perspective of the major stakeholder groups.

Internal stakeholder economic viability

When undertaking any conventional property appraisal for private investment purposes, whether in connection with proposed development or redevelopment or for other purposes, the effects of the building on other parties, economic or otherwise, are ignored. The concerns of different internal stakeholder sub-groups differ and it is useful to consider these as follows.

The investors' or owners' views

The investor will normally, but not always, seek direct pecuniary gain.(6) The criteria on which value is calculated in the hands of the investor will vary, but for most the following headings will be taken into account.

- The location;
- The tenure (such as freehold or leasehold);
- The tenancy-legal occupier contract;

- The identity and perceived quality of the tenant;
- The building's physical characteristics, including design and specification; and
- The investment return in the hands of the owner, usually expressed as a yield which links the income to the capital value (in relation to rental and capital growth valuation expectations).

It is often taken as a truism that location is a key determinant of economic value, but as previously explained public transport and other publicly funded infrastructure may be essential for a location to be successful. The desirability of a location is also associated with its proximity to markets.

While this is important for most types of building it is particularly so for wealth consuming buildings, notably retail units, where even fifty metres can significantly affect value in the hands of the occupier. Over time (see Box 3.4) the quality of a location changes with the influence of fashion, marketing, technological change and demographic trends. Fiscal and legislative actions can also affect the quality of a location: for example, the imposition of higher petrol tax may affect discretionary journey lengths and measures such as congestion changing will affect the attractiveness of some locations. An initial assessment of the Congestion Charge in London suggests that it may have had an adverse effect on some retail locations such as Oxford Street, that lie within the zone.

The tenure of any investment is important. Freehold, leasehold or a private finance initiative structure may influence the investment value, preventing (or allowing) the investor to enjoy income and capital growth. A leasehold tenure of 999 years, despite its length, may inhibit the use of a building in a way that does not apply with a freehold tenure.

Income derived from any investment may be determined by the contract with the occupier tenant – rent payer of that investment. The structure and nature of that tenancy contract, or lease or license will have a bearing on the economic viability of that investment.

From an investor's viewpoint the tenant's covenant will also influence value. A strong covenant will reduce the element of default risk

Oxford Street, London
This street is a major international retail and tourism destination, which has a world-renowned location giving instant 'brand recognition' for the occupier, thus supporting long-term economic success.

County Hall, London
Originally built for the London County Council, with the demise of its successor the Greater London Council, this prestigious headquarters building became redundant. It offered a range of opportunities, including of course a major office tenant, but possibly few would have anticipated the conversion to a multi-occupied building housing hotels, aquarium, family entertainment, art galleries, health club and a number of other uses. It is now a key element in the regeneration of the river frontage from here to Shad Thames to the east.

Tate Modern Art Gallery, London
This is housed in a disused coal-fired electricity generating station on the south bank of the Thames. Having stood empty for many years in a location suffering economic decline the emerging tourist trail along the South Bank from County Hall to Shad Thames has redefined the area and the building has proved successful in terms of scale and flexibility for its new role.

Architects Herzog and de Meuron Architecture Studio

Box 3.5: The Circle of Blame

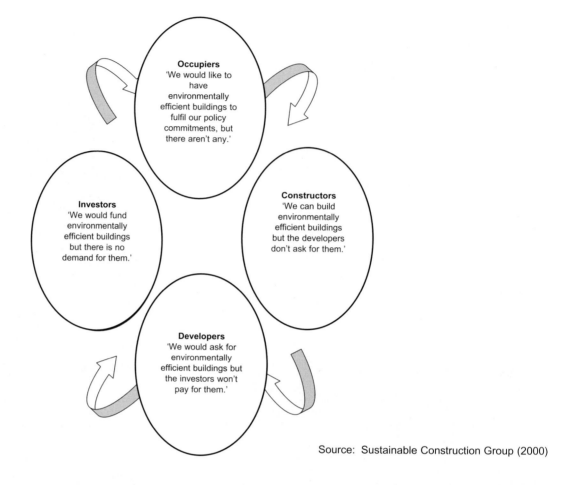

Source: Sustainable Construction Group (2000)

which is important in any situation, but especially where either the location or the type of building is not likely to appeal to many other potential occupiers.

The design and configuration of the building can have a major influence on the future prospects for the investment. A building that will continue to have tenant appeal across a wide range of potential users is more likely to perform well economically. Over the last decade, with a shift in planning policy encouraging modern town centre developments, many mixed use buildings have been constructed, typically incorporating retail, leisure and residential, where the complexity of form may detract from their future adaptability.

Baum (1994) makes a connection in relation to offices between the innate quality of a building and its investment performance. In this regard, the concepts of aesthetics, cost in use and function may, as previously discussed, have an important part to play in investment analysis. Little research work has been done to test this contention systematically, although some work in the United States in the 1980s provides limited evidence of a link (Brennan *et al.*, 1984; Vandell and Lane, 1989).

Although a link can be established between building quality and investment value, the nature of commercial lease patterns within the UK has tended to weaken it and thus the sustainability of the building in terms of environmental and social criteria has not been important in the decision making process. This has been shown by the so-called 'circle of blame' (7) in which the apparent lack of interest in 'green' buildings by investors has frustrated many in the construction sector.

The standard UK lease agreement requires that the tenant take over all responsibility for repairs and maintenance and rents are normally agreed in such a way that they cannot fall in actual terms. Until recently with terms being normally for up to

Godalming, Surrey
The successful application of a building for a modern food and beverage outlet has benefited from the historic context which provides the ambience for leisure while the space had the degree of flexibility appropriate for the use.

25 years, and in some cases longer, (8) the physical characteristics of the building became of little concern to investors, provided that an initial letting could be achieved. The introduction of a new Commercial Lease Code in 2002 (www. commercialleasecodeew.co.uk) developed by the major property organisations (including RICS, British Property Federation, NACORE and others) working together with government and a threat of legislation if it is not taken up by investors, may once more produce a connection between the investor and the building design in a more meaningful way than has been apparent over the last three decades.

Finally, the investor needs to consider how all the above factors influence the investment yield (the relationship between the rental value and capital value) and the prospects for rental and capital growth. Economic sustainability for the investment rests on the premise that investors are looking for two elements of; the income received from the investment and capital growth. This may be derived either from growth in the rental value and/or a change in the investment yield of the original acquisition value. For example, if an investment has a 10% income yield at purchase and, without the income changing, the yield falls to 8% there will be a 20% capital gain.

Ultimately, the investment yield will depend upon:

- the expected economic demand for the particular building in its particular location over time;
- the total volume of investor demand for properties: a function of comparative risks and returns and the wider investment market.

Where the building investor is also the occupier, the notion of investment return is interpreted differently as the capital employed in the building is usually viewed in relation to the whole business enterprise.

The occupiers' viewpoint

From a building occupier's perspective, there are four essential elements determining value in relation to their use of a building. These are:

- location,
- functional efficiency,
- aesthetic considerations, and
- costs in use.

Collectively, these factors will drive both the level of demand and the rental bid. While the residential sector may be driven by aspects of aesthetics and

Building conversion

Many residential care homes have in the past operated in converted Victorian and Edwardian houses. The changes in legislation in respect of minimum room sizes have forced some out of business. This building in Reigate, Surrey has been converted from a care home to flats.

location, to the commercial occupier, it is more likely that location and functionality are the prime consideration.

The **location** of a building has been discussed from the point of view of the investor viewpoint and it is equally true from the perspective of the occupier. Indeed value in the hands of the investor in this regard mimics the concern of the occupier as the investor seeks to establish the likely tenant demand.

Ultimately the viability of any building (both financial and non-financial) depends upon the functional demands of the user. Building **functionality** will therefore change over time as their requirements or those of the legislation which controls their activities changes. Thus value relates not only to how the building can be used now, but

also to its ability to accommodate changes in working practices over time. Building flexibility and form are important elements functional sustainability of the occupier's activities. An analysis of functionality can be applied equally to an office, a factory, an educational or religious building, but as stated earlier, wealth-creating uses are more sensitive to functional efficiency than wealth-consuming or cultural buildings.

With increases in social legislation (for example, the Disability Discrimination Act) financial viability may in some cases be lost. Over time changes in the economy and technological advances also have a significant influence on the occupational viability of a building.

The **aesthetics** or the loveability of any building will influence the occupier's value judgement.

Aesthetic appeal can enhance an occupier's status as well as providing a 'feel-good' factor. Such an appreciation is not restricted to any specific use and applies to a greater or lesser extent to a church, a cinema, a home, a shop or an office. In their annual report, English Heritage (English Heritage, 2002) state '*The historic environment enriches the quality of our lives. As a result, it is a major economic asset*'. However, the connection between aesthetic and economic value is not usually transparent within the property appraisal process.

The **cost in use** of the building determines whether in its own right, or as a factor of the users production process, it is likely to be sustainable. Again both commercial and non-commercial users will need to consider this aspect (see for example, Clift and Bourke, 1999). Much research has been undertaken in relation to the prediction of costs in use over time and the case has been promoted that buildings which comply with the principles of good environmentalism as set out in the BREEAM guides, (9) are economic in the hands of the occupier. These can vary substantially according to the occupiers expectations for the standards of maintenance.

However, to the business operator, the savings in costs of both maintenance and management which are due to building design are small compared with the overall costs of the business itself. An office occupier in central London may, for example, be paying £650 per m^2 in rent and almost half as much again in property taxation and other outgoings. When the costs of staffing and general business overheads are included, the costs in use relating to energy use and efficiency of £30 per m^2 per annum for example become of very little significance (Sayce *et al.*, 2001). It follows that the **cost in use** criterion for occupiers is connected more closely to matters of location and business practice than to building specification, adding further to the 'circle of blame' (see Box 3.5). Research (Capital Economics, 2002) has demonstrated that commercial property occupiers often do not operate their buildings efficiently, but this did not enhance the case for 'green buildings' on economic grounds.

The developer's viewpoint

In a market economy, one of the simplest ways to understand whether a building is economically sustainable and should be retained and refurbished or demolished, is to consider the residual land value which may or may not arise from new development. This however ignores the longer-term economic performance as well as social and environmental sustainability and while the latter will be of less importance to the developer the former will be fundamental to the building's future.

Box 3.6 provides sample conventional appraisals of a redundant building for which redevelopment or refurbishment are options under consideration. In these simple valuations the refurbished building has a lower lettable area and market perception commands a higher investment yield (reflecting the higher maintenance risk), resulting in a lower capital value and a negative residual land value of £3,100.

In contrast, the new building is more efficient in terms of net lettable area, may have floor plates that offer greater efficiency in use and can therefore command a higher rent. There is also a market perception is that it has a lower manage-ment risk, resulting in a lower capitalisation yield and hence a higher capital value.

This results in a positive rather than negative residual land value (of £750) despite the expenditure on refurbishment in the previous calculation being lower than the cost of constructing a new building.

The example quoted is simplistic, since the decision whether to refurbish or redevelop depends on building density and useable floor space created. If an increased density of development or better quality of space can be achieved, economic returns are likely to be enhanced. So an existing building that is not optimising its site cover is at greater economic risk than one which has a density in excess of planning expectations for new development (Scanlon *et al.*, 2003).

This simple private market calculation fails however to take into account any calculation in relation to energy consumption and the building's wider environmental or social impact. BRE, through their 'Office Scorer' programme have produced guidance on the environmental impact (10) involved in the decision to redevelop or refurbish but only in relation to offices.

Undoubtedly useful as a mechanism for assessing overall environmental sustainability from an external stakeholder and user perspective,

Box 3.6: Office building appraisals

		£	£
Residual Valuation: Refurbishment			
Gross Area	100		
Net Lettable/Useable	70		
Let @ £7 psf p.a.	7	490	
YP in perp @ 10%			4,900
Refurbishment			
Cost @ £80 psf			
(including finance)			8,000
Land Value Residual			**(3,100)**
Residual Valuation: New Building			
Gross Area	100		
Net Lettable/Useable	85		
Let @ £12 psf p.a.	12	1,020	
YP in per @ 8%		12.5	12,750
New Build			
Cost @ £120 psf			12,000
(including demolition finance)			
Land Value Residual			**750**

it does not assist in assessing economic viability in the hands of the developer. The developer may well develop and walk away from the building, possibly selling on to an investor, who also lacks any meaningful incentive to incorporate the triple bottom line criteria. It has been the rise in the Corporate Social Responsibility agenda amongst building stakeholders rather than the energy efficiency argument that is the potential driving force.

The external stakeholder's perspective

In Chapter 1 the key concept of the 6 'Ls' of sustainability is outlined. Each has an economic inference and if there is a fundamental conflict between the economic considerations of internal stakeholders and the wider sustainability criteria (especially viewed from the external perspective) then the future life of the buildings will be at risk.

From the external stakeholders' point of view, the economic interest they have in connection with a building in which they have no direct pecuniary interest is likely to be marginal. They may have some wider concerns. For example in a commercial area the efficiency of a particular building may affect the economic success or otherwise of neighbouring retail outlets, affect the pedestrian footfall and thus retail turnover which then feeds through to employment in the sector and the promotion of economic vitality in the area. Similarly, the ability of businesses to operate efficiently in the buildings they occupy will ultimately feed through to the costs of the services they provide.

The investment return of a building in the hands of an investor or owner-occupier has been shown to be critical. Where investment returns are too low to generate profitable activity in terms of property investment, urban degradation may follow. This in turn, if it requires public sector gap funding to 'kick-start' activity, has a cost to external stakeholders.

The efficiency of land use and the density of existing buildings are highlighted as developer's factors. From the external economic perspective, the most efficient use of land may improve accessibility and the promotion of high density can reduce travel costs to and from the building. It may however have a cost in terms of congestion.

A summary of issues and moves to economic sustainability

At the beginning of this chapter it was argued that economic sustainability, which is assumed to be a goal in its own right, is best assured by adopting full TBL principles.

This is the argument that has been made forcefully in relation the construction and property industries (Sustainable Construction Task Group, 2001). They argue that adopting good TBL principles will provide companies with:

- *Strategic benefits*, such as enhanced reputation leading to the ability to improve their credit rating, attract high quality staff and reduce the risks associated with non-compliance with environmental legislation;
- *Operational benefits*, such as reducing liability for Climate Change levy and landfill tax; and
- *Revenue-generating benefits*, such as the ability to attract more clients or, in the case of investors, funds and the production of more flexible and attractive properties.

This list of perceived benefits has implications for building owners, occupiers, and developers. It recognises the role of buildings within the corporate portfolio as assets that are representative of the core values for which both owner and occupier stand. It requires an analysis of properties in terms of their contribution to the TBL as well as the single goal of profit.

When individual stakeholder views are analysed however, it can be seen that the concept of economic viability is largely driven by the single bottom line of profit: the 'business of business is to stay in business' argument. The matter of economic sustainability is wider and needs to take into account both private and public concepts of economic well-being. It must be seen in the context of the triple bottom line and has thus to take account of social and environmental concerns.

The *Buildings: a new life* project revealed through dialogue questionnaire and case studies, a number of issues that are considered critical to determining whether or not a building should be retained or given a new life.

In economic terms, these centre on building efficiency in terms of configuration, adaptability and location. For the investor the ability of the building to attract tenants of high standing is equally important. The issues of energy efficiency and ecological concerns do not rank highly with internal stakeholders.

In the next two chapters the concepts of environmental and social sustainability are developed. Below is a summary of issues that affect the economic sustainability of a building and which should form the basic agenda for discussion in using the BSAT detailed in Chapter 6.

- Is the building form and fabric such that continued life is feasible without public subsidy?
- Does the building work efficiently in the hands of the occupier?
- Is the building adaptable within 'reasonable cost' parameters?
- Does the building show private economic rates of return, or could it do so?
- Does the current building, and its actual or potential use, represent an efficient use of the land?
- Is economic sustainability hampered or aided by the tenure relationships?
- Are the location and accessibility, including public transport accessibility appropriate for continued use and exploitation of the building?

Consideration of the issues set out above leads to some key questions for discussion regarding the future life of an existing commercial building. These questions are not regarded as either exclusive or limiting – the very nature of buildings means that individual factors may require additional debates to take place. They are offered as a standard template or minimum set of issues that will arise in almost ever case and are set out at the end of Chapter 6 setting out the use of the BSAT.

Endnotes

1   The templates for Quality of Life Indicators have been
    revised since they were first published to accommodate

the results of pilot implementation. The 2002 templates contain 38 indicators, of which 5 only are economic (Audit Commission 2002).

2 For example the Roskill Commission in its study of a third London Airport as long ago as 1971 famously put a 'shadow price' on the value of a Saxon Church in an attempt to appropriately price in the cost of destruction.

3 Much of the postwar housing was anticipated to have a maximum life of 15 years but some examples have survived to be protected by listing. The development of prefabrication during this period is examined in detail in *Prefabrication* by White RB, HMSO, 1965.

4 Currently there are some 500,000 listed buildings.

5 For example, the building of the Jubilee Line Extension has been observed to have radically affected the land values surrounding the new transport nodes (Riley, 2001). On a smaller scale, the building of a town by-pass may enhance *residential* values, while leading to *decline* for some other uses (for example petrol filling stations and wayside pubs and restaurants).

6 It is outside the scope of this work to develop these criteria in detail. Readers wishing a more detailed exploration are pointed to, for example, Baum and Crosby (1995), Isaac (1998) and Hoesli and Macgregor (2000).

7 This term was coined by the Sustainable Construction Task Group (2000) – see Box 3.6.

8 The 'institutional lease' of 25 years with 5-years upward-only rent reviews and a complete transfer to the tenant of all liabilities held sway from the early 1970s until the mid 1990s. Indeed, many new leisure park units constructed in the early to mid 1990s saw even longer terms (up to 35 years) agreed with even more onerous terms to include guaranteed uplift on rents at review.

9 The reader is pointed to BREEAM as published by the Building Research Establishment (BRE) (www.bre.co.uk). The BRE publication, *A Sustainability Checklist for Developments* provides a useful overview of the ambitions for *new* buildings.

10 'Office Scorer' considers the impact of both refurbishment and redevelopment options in terms of heating, lighting, ventilation and embodied impacts. It also considers the density of use.

Chapter 4

Environmental Sustainability of Buildings

Principal Messages:

- *Environmental sustainability is concerned with the conservation of natural resources, the avoidance of pollution, the minimising of waste and the protection of bio-diversity. It is also concerned with the reduction in activities believed to contribute to global warming.*

- *Energy consumption is considered to be a major environmental issue both because of fossil fuel depletion and for its contribution to carbon emissions, which in turn are linked to global warming.*

- *In the UK energy consumption is of special importance to buildings since they take up to 50% of all energy consumed compared with 25% each in industry and transport. It is estimated that up to 90% of building energy is consumed in use rather than construction, but that energy use in buildings is wasteful with up to 75% capable of being saved by simple improvements.*

- *There are many other considerations in relation to the environmental sustainability of buildings including minimising waste, location factors and many other user considerations.*

- *New buildings represent only 2% of our building stock and determining the fate of an existing building brings many other factors into play including the occupiers' understanding of and commitment to a sustainable environment on a global scale.*

- *During the life cycle of a building, the interests of different stakeholder groups can sometimes conflict and the capital costs of meeting environmental objectives may not be reflected in benefits or returns for those responsible for the expenditure.*

- *The objective in this chapter is to identify some of the different and potentially conflicting issues which need to be considered and to help owners, users and the wider community to understand the issues to be addressed.*

Environmental sustainability is just one part of the triple bottom line and of no greater importance than social or economic issues; however in some ways this has proved an area with which it has been easier for commentators to identify and also more susceptible to measurement especially for issues such as energy consumption. The result has been a significant body of work on environmental sustainability issues and thus of necessity this chapter is of greater substance in order to cover the range of issues which have been researched. It has been approached at two levels with the first half of the chapter examining the wider global concerns and then in the second half considering their application to the specific building context.

A definition of Environmental Sustainability

Environmental Sustainability relates to matters concerned with planetary protection and the maintenance of diverse eco-systems. It requires both a detailed knowledge of the earth's 'carrying capacity' and the adaptation of economic and human activity to that which can be sustained. While many have attempted to establish what is environmentally sustainable no complete agreement has been reached as to what actions are appropriate or necessary.

The following quote provides a sobering thought and depicts the scale of the issue. *'Humankind has inherited a 3.8 billion-year store of natural capital. At present rates of use and degradation, there will be little left by the end of the next century'* (Hawken, Lovins and Lovins, 1999:3). To Hawken and his colleagues, the challenge of environmental sustainability is concerned primarily with the rate of depletion of natural resources – it is a matter of non-renewable resources being consumed with increasing rapidity. To them and to many others the issue is a race of technology against depletion and, where practical, replenishment.

Before examining the specific issues related to buildings an overview is necessary of the global environmental issues.

Environmental degradation

Some of the key physical manifestations of the 'environmental problem' which have particular relevance to buildings are shown below.

Ozone depletion

Attention has been focused on the depletion of ozone at high levels and the anticipated global warming which will arise from the loss of this natural protective layer which can lead to increased incidence of skin cancer, eye complaints, and damage to crops. In the lower atmosphere ozone, a compound of oxygen widely used in the bleaching and purifying industries, is a pollutant which is damaging to plants and human beings. Ironically the trees which can do so much to remove contaminants, carbon dioxide and other gasses, can also emit volatile organic compounds (VOCs) into the atmosphere which enter into chemical reactions in sunlight with oxides of nitrogen produced by fossil fuel combustion to form ozone and other products (Centre for Ecology & Hydrology, Lancashire University).

A key factor leading to ozone depletion is the use of chlorofluorocarbons (CFCs); these are widely used in the building industry in foam plastics as well as in refrigeration plant and in many cases they can be replaced by hydro fluorocarbons which are less damaging. Legislation is now controlling their use, but this introduces a waste management problem since obsolete plant must be disposed of and can place a restriction on the subsequent use of landfill sites for many years.

Global warming

Global warming is believed by many already to have caused significant climate changes, which are likely to grow unless the underlying factors are addressed within a comparatively short time-scale. It is caused by emission of the so-called 'greenhouse gases': water vapour, Carbon Dioxide (CO_2), Methane (CH_4), Nitrous Oxide (N_2O), and halocarbons CFC11 and CFC12. The most important of these is CO_2 which is emitted in the production of electricity from fossil fuels as well as from other processes. Although all these gases can occur naturally, their emissions have been enormously increased by man's activities, the use of buildings and their plant and through traffic generation.

The situation is aggravated by deforestation which not only gives rise to a loss of species and land erosion but also through a reduction of vegetation leads to CO_2 not being re-absorbed by plants as part of the carbon cycle.

Carbon is a key element for the sustainability of life on earth. The carbon cycle provides a balanced eco-system where the carbon embodied in plant and animal life is released slowly into the atmosphere after death and decomposition, taken up by plants and returned to the animal food chain. An imbalance at any stage such as an artificially increased rate of carbon release, will disrupt the cycle and have wider implications for the maintenance of a balanced environment. To put this in context, every kilowatt hour of electricity used in the UK releases 1 kilogram of CO_2.

Table 4.1: Carbon Dioxide emissions

Year	% Atmosphere
1900	0.028
2000	0.035

Source: Intergovernmental Panel on Climate Change((www.ipcc.ch)

An increase in carbon dioxide leads to an increase in atmospheric water vapour, creating greater climatic change and meteorological instability. This volatility, and its impact on global warming, will create more droughts and flooding (such as in Prague during 2002) and will result in sea levels rising as the polar ice caps melt which could lead to the problems shown below.

Table 4.2: Flooding: high risk regions

Venice, Italy
Tokyo, Japan
South Texas, USA
Bangkok, Thailand
Abu Dhabi, UAE
Dubai, UAE
London, UK
Netherlands
New York, USA

Source: Morrell (2001)

It is interesting that the cities which have grown the fastest in recent years, either in terms of population or of wealth (or both), are often those cities which are the most vulnerable to changes in global environment and therefore for whose inhabitants the issues of global warming may be most relevant.

Table 4.3: Temperature: global deviation from average degrees Celsius

1860	−0.4
1880	−0.2
1900	−0.2
1920	−0.3
1940	−0.05
1960	0.0
1980	0.0
2000	+0.4

Source: Intergovernmental Panel on Climate Change (www.ipcc.ch)

The major problems associated with global warming are:

- **Climate change**, which is occurring at a rate sufficient to affect the ecological balance
- **Flooding and violent weather patterns**, which again affect the areas of land suitable

for development and the types of building which would be sustainable for these locations.

Both of these have an impact on the type and nature of developments possible and of course have a knock-on effect on insurance of buildings and their value.

Fossil fuel depletion

The UK is still dependent on fossil fuel with less than 10% of its energy being obtained from renewable sources, such as water, wind and solar power. Nuclear power is claimed by the French generating industry to be a true eco-friendly form of electricity production since it has none of the emissions associated with global pollution; however this is an instance where inter-generational issues must be considered since the long term disposal of waste at present creates environmental risks of a considerable magnitude.

In many ways this dependence on fossil fuels is extraordinary given that the UK has a long coast line with a high tidal range and an extensive river system thus giving huge potential for hydro-electricity, a very windy climate allowing for wind power and sufficient sunlight to make photovoltaics a practical option for significant energy generation. Whatever the reasons, and in part it arises from the historical abundance of coal in the UK, the exploitation of renewables, while technically practicable, has been under utilised. The UK government is committed to a policy of achieving 10% of power by renewable sources by 2010 and has announced proposals for off shore windfarms to be developed around the coasts.

Fossil fuel depletion leads to two requirements:

- The need to reduce fuel consumption where this is based on fossil fuels;
- The need to ensure that alternative sources of power are utilised wherever possible.

Within the building supply chain industry there is widespread awareness of the issue and the whole Building Best Practice scheme is geared towards promoting these aims. There is concern however that new buildings in the commercial or residential sectors are seldom specified to meet the needs of energy reduction and the August 2003 revisions to section L of the Building Regulations go only partway to address this issue. The Latham Report (1994) and the Sustainable Construction Task Force (2002) advocate green construction and identify barriers, including lack of knowledge and a 'circle of blame' with each party saying they are signed up to the Agenda but that others are not!

Progress is being made with many new buildings now achieving high BREEAM (Building Research Establishment Environmental Assessment Method) ratings, but they are still in the minority. BREEAM rates buildings on a range of issues relating to their construction and ability to be managed in compliance with environmental principles taking on board issues such as waste disposal, the location of the building and 'green' travel plans.

Acid rain

Acid rain is caused by polluting emissions in heavy industrial areas, and is typical of a 'trans-boundary' problem. Some areas of Eastern Europe in particular are very badly affected and the situation is aggravated by inefficient processes. The effects include the destruction of vegetation, important not only to agriculture, but also to tourism and climatic balance. It is not a problem widely associated with the UK.

Polluted and contaminated land

Polluted and contaminated land is mainly, though not exclusively, the product of our industrial past resulting from industrial processes and landfill. The size of the problem in the UK is uncertain but it has been estimated that up to 50,000 ha are affected, depending on the particular definition of contamination used. The methods for dealing with contaminated land vary depending on the nature of the contaminant. In some cases it can be satisfactorily dealt with by covering, or by complete encapsulation, but at other times soil cleaning is required. In this case waste management is a major issue including the associated transport requirements.

Contaminants may:

- attach to and be contained within the ground;
- flow in the water and thereby migrate onto adjoining land;
- be airborne gases which result from activity on the ground.

Contamination can occur through:

- natural problems
- mineral extraction or processing
- land fill activity
- farming (both arable and husbandry)
- chemical contaminants.

Although the most common sources of contamination arise from the industrial legacy (e.g. iron and steel working, tanneries, etc) they may relate to modern processes too (explosives, electricity substations, railway premises, chemical productions, etc).

Current government policy is to insist that development increasingly takes place on brown-field sites. Some of these may have little contamination; others are heavily polluted and this seriously affects the financial viability of such developments, especially if stigma becomes associated with the site or location. Accordingly it is important that allowances for 'clean-up' is both worked in to the appraisal and that the level and type of decontamination is appropriate to the consequent use. For example, the clean-up technology employed and level of decontamination required is very different for residential use as opposed to a sports ground or an industrial part. Residential development, for which government is seeking substantial reuse of brown-field sites, requires the highest level of clean-up.

Sick buildings

The term 'sick building syndrome' was coined in the 1970s in response to problems arising in sealed buildings with in adequate mechanical ventilation systems (Brandt, 1994). A variety of factors including harmful chemical emissions from carpets and other building materials, combined with occasional pathogens breeding in the constantly recycled air in the ventilation systems, caused illness amongst the building occupants. Probably the most notorious were the outbreaks of Legionnaires Disease, which is water-borne and is often caused by poorly designed or maintained air-conditioning or water cooling plant and could affect not only the buildings occupants but also passers-by. Poor lighting or lack of visual contact with the outside can also contribute to the lack of well being and with staff productivity being an issue to many employers a building that is seen to contribute to lack of productivity may have a lower value. Evidence from America indicates that a green building provides a more productive workplace – at least a 1% increase in productivity – and thus an economically more sustainable building, but there is little systematic evidence to confirm this for the UK so far (Edwards, 1998).

Water or air pollution

Air pollution can be caused by building use and process emission and by traffic emissions. The types of pollution include sulphur dioxide, lead, carbon dioxide and particulates. Traffic pollution is a major problem that is being tackled primarily through planning legislation. The poor quality of air and high pollen counts, which can be aggravated by particulate pollution, have significantly increased the number of breathing related ailments including asthma.

Water pollution, caused by run-off from agricultural chemicals, sewage and industrial discharges is also a growing problem, although the work of the Environment Agency has been at least partially successful in reducing water pollution.

Radon gas and other naturally occurring substances

Radon gas is normally associated with areas of old hard rocks however it is widely distributed throughout the UK. Its escape can be very damaging to health (lung cancer in particular). The risk of radon being present can be identified by desktop study and where the risk is high more detailed surveys will be required under the Building Regulations with appropriate steps taken to prevent ingress into a building or a build up of pockets of the gas.

Other substances, such as mercury, may occur naturally and give the appearance of contamination by man's activities, even where this is not the case.

These issues are now examined in more detail specifically related to buildings and their implications for the different stakeholder groups.

Application of the issues to buildings

There are three stages in the life of a building: (i) conception and construction, (ii) use and (iii)

demolition or decay. Sir Richard Rogers has put it more imaginatively in saying that this process of manufacture, erection, maintenance and demolition provides the 'how, why and what' of the building, the legibility which gives it scale, grain and shadow' (Sudjic, 1986). However it is described, account must be taken at all stages of the objectives and the inherent environmental constraints if building sustainability is to be achieved.

The challenge in terms of the building life cycle with which this guide is primarily concerned is in recognising the point at which the building is no longer viable within a triple bottom line context. With a single environmental factor such as energy use, it is a comparatively simple quantitative exercise to establish the energy credentials of different options, by using tools such as BRE's Envest (www.bre.co.uk). Such tools however normally apply primarily to new buildings and do not present a holistic view of environmental factors or the TBL.

It must be recognised that environmental demands can be a source of conflict in the search for sustainable solutions to the question of whether or not to retain a building. The embodied energy (in simple terms the energy which was required to create the building originally or the energy which would be involved in its replacement) of an existing building will generally make it desirable to retain the structure so as to increase the period over which the environmental costs can be amortised, but that may well conflict with the efficient use of the accommodation and its consumption of energy in occupation.

The argument may be easier to comprehend if we consider that the future potential life of the building that should be balanced against the embodiment of energy involved in redevelopment or refurbishment.

Because of the related CO_2 emissions, energy consumption (as opposed to embodied energy) is undoubtedly first among the environmental sustainability issues highlighting the tensions between the external stakeholder community, which has a vested interest in reducing energy consumption, and the building user for whom the use of energy is perceived as a business cost and one that is small generally compared with other costs such as staffing and rent.

Box 4.1 Embodied energy as a case for building retention

English Heritage (2002) has suggested that the brickwork in a standard Victorian terrace property has an embodied energy equivalent to 30,000 litres of petrol or about 250,000 miles for an average car. On that basis it might be better to retain existing structures even if their viability relies on the use of private transport. For a simple house the ratio of the embodied energy required to create the building to the total energy consumed over a 75-year period is only about 15:100, but with increasing efficiency in energy use, or for buildings with a shorter life cycle, the proportion attributed to embodied energy will rise significantly and we can therefore see how embodied energy may become increasingly significant in determining the sustainability of a building.

Apart from conserving energy there are a number of other issues which contribute to the environmental sustainability of a building. Whether the proposal is for redevelopment or retention with maintenance and possible refurbishment consideration must be given to building materials and products, as well as waste and water management and the impact on ecology. Important too, are matters such as the quality of the space (for example in relation to natural day lighting), its adaptability for the user and whether or not it provides a healthy working environment, including issues related to sick buildings.

There are therefore a series of topics to be considered, all of which may to some extent be taken as measures of the efficient use of natural and manufactured resources and therefore of concern to both external and internal stakeholders. Some of these are of greater immediate significance than others and evaluating their relative impact helps in setting priorities. According to Redland Roofing (2002) the issues can be ranked as follows:

Primary importance:	energy use and CO_2 emissions rate (57%)
Second:	resource depletion and waste (24%)
Third:	toxic emissions in air (13%) and
Fourth:	pollution (7%)

While there are inevitable conflicts of interest between internal and external stake-holders, they are probably less noticeable when considering environmental issues since all stakeholders are equally likely to have a common interest in the global welfare of the environment.

Notwithstanding this, the internal stakeholders must balance the environmental considerations against their personal and corporate costs in a way that external stakeholders do not. The conflicts need to be recognised and resolved in order to proceed to appropriate decisions. There is little incentive to improve the environmental controls outlined below if they represent capital expenditure for no financial return. For example it has been shown that fuel from rapeseed oil is as efficient and causes significantly less pollution than traditional fuel oils but since it costs twice as much there is little prospect of its being used unless there is a public subsidy or an imposed penalty.

It has been suggested that 'green' adaptations incorporated into a building will pay for themselves. Edwards (1998) argued strongly that most green buildings are economic, but went on say that poor green design may lead to expenditure which can never be recovered. Some of the predicted savings such as switching off lights are not achieved in practice because of lack of commitment on the part of the user (Smith, 2001).

To obtain a benefit from the many sophisticated methods of controlling a building's environment, it is essential that the occupiers take over ownership of the processes and the objectives. In an artificial environment the occupier will tend to expect greater reliance on automated means of environmental control and is demonstrably less interested in optimising the performance of the building (Smith, 2001). Controls which are too complex will be ignored or overridden and could even lead to earlier obsolescence: the human factor takes over and the savings which have been anticipated may fail to materialise.

From the above we can see that in order to assess the environmental sustainability of a building it is necessary to balance issues with detailed factual data and benchmark examples against others with only a subjective qualitative assessment.

The following sections provide an indicator to some of the key issues to be considered and, together with the bibliography, will help to identify sources of further information.

Energy: the issue

At present sustainable forms of energy production form only a small proportion (15–20% of the European Union demand by 2020) of the total energy consumed but as this balance changes so the focus on energy conservation may become less important than other issues in assessing sustainability. The white paper issued in February 2003 (DTI, 2003) set targets and includes the implementation of the EU Directive on Energy Performance in Buildings (EU, 2002). The latter proposes certificates of energy performance for new and existing buildings which must be renewed every five years and requirements such as the inspection of all plant such as boilers over a certain age. This may highlight the different interests of the building owner, occupier and community as while the former is likely to have to fund any energy conservation measures, any running cost benefits accrue to the second and overall environmental benefits to the last group.

Lovelock (2000 [a] and [b]) makes the point that the total energy used for a building must take into account not only that used in its construction and in its running and maintenance, but also that used by the occupiers in travelling to and from the building during its lifetime. Conventionally this is not included in a building appraisal.

Although there are a number of other gases which can be taken into account including methane, nitrous oxide and halocarbons, it is carbon dioxide which is increasingly important in environmental terms because of the increased proportion in the atmosphere.

It is clear that there is a need to reduce CO_2 emissions and there is a general consensus that buildings are major contributors at every stage of their life cycle but from the table below it can be seen clearly that energy consumption comes very low on the list of total running costs, and that unless there is some degree of compulsion or real benefit, saving energy is unlikely to be a priority for the building user.

Table 4.4: Office costs: people, buildings and energy

Salaries	130
Gross Office Rent	21
Total Energy	1.81
(of which Electricity	1.53)
Repair & Maintenance	1.37

Source: Hawken *et al.* (1999)

Even the simplest decisions such as those of insulation are affected by other factors such as the form of the building. For a single storey building the roof and its thermal performance will be a key element in the performance of the building as a whole, while for one of the proposed new skyscrapers the performance of the walls will be of far greater significance.

As building design becomes more efficient so energy costs are potentially reduced for new buildings and thus the cost of energy in use is unlikely to be a decisive factor between new construction or the retention of an old building.

The situation is often complicated further in commercial buildings by the different interests of occupier and owner. While the capital costs of improving the situation will be borne by the developer or owner, any benefits will accrue to the tenant and are currently unlikely to be sufficient to make any difference to the rent paid. Serviced offices and owner occupied spaces will not of course face this problem although the cost as a small proportion of the total still remains an issue.

Recent surveys of occupation costs, particularly for offices, indicate a wide variation ranging from 1735 euros per m^2 London, to 880 euros in Paris and 687 euros in New York for prime offices. A survey by Jones Lang LaSalle indicates that the service charge cost (of which energy use is a very small part) ranges from 105 euros for a London air-conditioned building down to 50 euros per m^2 for a regional city building without air conditioning. Direct energy costs (on heating and lighting) range from 8.00 euros per m^2 down to only 5.00 euros per m^2 or less. This again reinforces the problem that energy consumption, whilst critical to sustainability, is not a major economic issue to building users.

Embodied energy

The idea of 'embodied energy' was conceived and developed in the late 1960s and early 1970s when researchers were concerned with the depletion of scarce fuel resources especially following the oil crisis of the early 1970s and it was one of the themes taken up by both Meadows (1972) and Goldsmith (1972).

Many definitions of embodied energy have been devised, each reflecting a different emphasis. All the definitions have in common an estimate of the energy needed to make materials available to consumers which includes the energy consumed in extracting the raw materials or recycling old material, in manufacture and delivery to the site. Howard (1996) discussed the concept of construction materials and restated the concept of embodied energy as the energy needed to obtain the raw materials, manufacture products or elements and transport them to the building site and erection in place. Howard further stated that: '*Embodied CO$_2$ is the CO$_2$ released as a consequence of the embodied energy in the materials, as well as any additional CO$_2$ released due to the chemistry of the manufacturing process*'.

From Howard's paper the following table provides a comparative framework of embodied CO$_2$.

Table 4.5: Embodied energy in different buildings

Construction Type	Embodied CO$_2$ Kg CO$_2$/M^2
Office	500–1000
House	800–1200
Flat	500–1000
Industrial	400–700
Road	130–650

Source: Howard (1996)

These results demonstrate that there is very large

Table 4.6: Materials and embodied energy

Material	Embodied energy
Coated steels	The embodied energy 180-290Mj/m^2 compares well with traditional materials. Providing a protective finish increases the embodied energy but is compensated for by increased life. Stainless steel manufactured from scrap material has an embodied energy of 33Mj/m^2 of which 20% is due to the collection and distribution processes.
Aluminium	Primary aluminium has a high embodied energy content of 550-920 Mj/m^2 while recycled aluminium is very low at 30-90 Mj/m^2, however these figures can be misleading since 60% of primary aluminium is produced by hydroelectricity which is a renewable source.
Copper	A Guide to Sustainable Roofing gives copper, aluminium and lead levels between 550 and 920 Mj/m^2 but the materials are used at different thickness' and the European Copper Roofing Campaign gives a .6mm sheet of copper an embodied value of 50 Mj/m^2 compared with stainless steel at 75 Mj/m^2 for .38mm or aluminium at 100 Mj/m^2 for .7mm thick.
Lead	Primary lead has a very high embodied energy in the range 2848-7663 Mj/m^2 but this drops to 150–403 Mj/m^2 for recycled material.
Zinc	Primary zinc is 50 Mj/m^2 but this drops even further to 2.5 for recycled material.
Clay	As might be expected of a fired material, the values are high at 270–430 Mj/m^2.
Slate	Transport and waste gives rates of 130–160 Mj/m^2.
Concrete	The processing is a low intensity one and the materials have an embodied energy of 40-90 Mj/m^2.
Timber shingles	Very low levels of energy in manufacture so there can be significant differences due to transport costs.
Felts and asphalt	Varies but generally mid range.
Membranes	A figure of 71 mega-joules kilogram indicates that a low square metre rate should be achieved.
Green roofs	This natural roofing has a very low embodied energy depending on transport and similar issues and the main determinant will be the values attributed to the waterproof layer and its protection.

Source: *Ecotech* (2003)

Table 4.7: Industry benchmarks for energy use

	Gas/Oil Consumption		Electricity Consumption		Emissions		Cost	
	Good practice KWh/m²	Typical practice KWh/m²	Good practice KWh/m²	Typical practice KWh/m²	Good practice Kg CO₂ M²	Typical practice Kg CO₂ M²	Good practice £/M²tfa	Typical practice £/M²tfa
Smaller office	79	151	33	54	33	59	3.50	6
Naturally ventilated open plan	79	151	54	85	44	75	4.50	7
Air conditioned Open plan	97	178	128	226	86	154	8	14
Headquarters	114	210	234	358	145	229	13	20

Source: Energy Use in Offices (ECON 19) (Energy Efficiency Best Practice Programme 1998) quoted in Wasterbusters Ltd (2000)

potential for saving embodied energy by appropriate design, specification and the construction process. It is therefore relevant when considering the question of refurbishment and renewal including the energy savings arising from the reuse of materials.

An examination of a typical building component such as roofing illustrates the complexity of the embodied energy issue. Similar tables for the same materials are included under recycling and pollution to provide a comparison of the issues for a common range of materials.

Embodied energy therefore represents the energy which would be wasted in discarding a building or creating a replacement. It is part of the assessment as to whether it is more effective to retain an existing structure or replace it with one which is more efficient in use. However its more immediate effect is in assessing the long term effectiveness of individual components such as the roof and the most suitable materials to be used.

In summary the issue of embodied energy is important such that Williamson and others have demonstrated that ignoring this aspect in rating studies such as HERS or SAP can lead to the promotion of systems which actually increase the total energy dedicated to the building (Williamson, 2003).

Energy in use

Energy in use has been researched in detail and the Building Research Establishment (www.bre.co.uk) provides many publications to help assess it. Additionally, *The Green Office Manual* (Wastebusters, 2000) discusses energy use in relation to buildings together with ways in which companies should consider how best to reduce energy consumption.

The above table provides a comparative framework of energy in use for four different types of office building, and provides a guide to carbon dioxide emissions. Clearly, a traditional air conditioned building would normally be far more demanding on energy than a small office building without air conditioning, but this may not always be the case and it is important to assess each situation carefully. In terms of new buildings, compliance with Building Regulations goes some way towards ensuring minimum levels of energy efficiency and in making decisions regarding retention or redevelopment, the risk of possible changes to existing regulations should be considered.

In 1999 the UK Government introduced the Climate Change Levy, a tax on the business use of energy, which can be recycled back to business mainly through a reduction in employers' National Insurance Contribution (NIC) for full time employees. A report by the Confederation of British Industry in 2002 found that this new tax discriminated against the manufacturing rather than the service sector, partly because of more part time employment and greater use of energy per manufacturing employee compared with the service sector. It ignored energy used in transportation to the place of employment. Despite this critical analysis, the introduction of a Climate Change Levy indicates an increasing awareness of this issue.

This brief discussion highlights the increasing attention to matters of energy use in relation to commercial buildings. So far the approach taken by government has been primarily one of information to encourage a responsible approach, attitudes are changing and the matter is now becoming of greater financial significance as fiscal measures are progressively introduced and strengthened.

Energy and travel

The third energy component which needs to be taken into account after embodied energy in construction and energy in use, is that used in travelling to and from a particular building.

The Green Office Manual also provides the framework for understanding this concept, based on work published buildings by the DETR.

Table 4.8: The Green Office Manual CO_2 emissions by transport mode – vehicle/km

Transport mode	CO_2 per km (kg)	Unit
Bus	1.28	Vehicle km
Petrol car	0.20	Vehicle km
Diesel car	0.12	Vehicle km

Source: DETR, 1999 quoted in Wastebusters, 2000

Table 4.9: The Green Office Manual CO_2 emissions by transport mode passenger/km

Transport mode	CO_2 per km (kg)	Unit
Short haul flight	0.18	Passenger km
Tube	0.11	Passenger km
Long haul flight	0.11	Passenger km
Train	0.06	Passenger km

Source: DETR, 1999 quoted in Wastebusters, 2000

In the above tables a bus (when carrying passengers) is far less demanding on CO_2 per person travelled, than a petrol driven car. Perhaps more unexpected is the fact that the carbon dioxide used to travel by underground railway per km is equal to that used on a long haul aircraft flight.

The relevance of this to the environmental sustainability of a building is that the location of a building and its accessibility by bus or rail may be as critical, if not more so, than its design for energy efficiency. This will of course depend on the intensity of use of the building and the number of visits that it generates. Accordingly, the issue of accessibility and location may be more critical for office and retail premises, but relatively unimportant for warehouses.

Application of energy criteria to a single building

The following tables give a framework for calculating the energy used in a typical building. The first example is based on a relatively new air-conditioned building built within a town.

In this calculation the data illustrated above has been used as a framework for calculating the embodied energy of 10m² of office construction which is approximately the floor area used by one individual working in a modern office building. A similar calculation is applied to energy used for 10 years for 10 m². It is assumed that this is a newly constructed building and that a large amount of embodied energy has therefore to be used in the construction process.

Finally an assessment is made relating to transport, where a number of assumptions must be made. Here it is assumed that 30% of the occupiers travel 20 km by bus in a normal working day, that 40% of the occupants (being in a town centre) travel by rail, and that the remaining 30% travel by car. For the purpose of the exercise it is also assumed that they travel an average 20 km a day over a normal working year of 240 days (Table 4.10).

These three estimates of energy consumed are calculated per person per 10 years. By adding together the embodied energy of construction of the building, the energy use of the building in terms of heating and lighting, and the energy used in transporting an individual, an estimate of the total energy per person can be made.

A similar calculation can be devised for a residential building. In the example which follows, (Table 4.11) an old converted apartment building (previously in industrial use) has been used.

Table 4.10: Energy use for an example commercial individual building – Kg CO_2 /10 m^2

Embodied Energy			10,000
Energy in use per m^2 p.a.	200		
Over 10 years			20,000
Transport Energy			
Bus per 1km per person	0.05		
Return Journey 20 km	1.00		
Percent by Bus	30%	0.30	
Days 240		72	
Trains per 1 km per person	0.11		
Return Journey 20km	2		
Percent by Train	40%	0.80	
Day 240		19.2	
Car per 1 km per person	0.20		
Return Journey 20km	4		
Percent by Car	30%	1.2	
Days 240		288	
Transport Total per year		379.2	
Over 10 years			3,792
Total Kg CO_2 10 m^2			33,792

Table 4.11: Embodied energy: Kg CO_2/10 m^2 over 10 years

Embodied Energy			2,000
Energy in use per m^2 p.a.	50		
Over 10 years			5,000
Transport Energy (Apartment – 50 m^2 per person)			
Bus per 1km person	0.05		
Average Journey per trip km	10		
Number of Days per year	365		
Percentage of Trips by Bus/Year	20%		
Total Bus per year		36.5	
Trains per 1km person	0.01		
Average Journey per trip km	100		
Number of Days per year	365		
Percentage of Trips Train/Year	10%		
Total Train per year		36.5	
Car per 1 km person	0.20		
Average Journey per trip km	50		
Days per year	365		
Percentage of Trip Car/Year	70%		
Total Car per year per person 50 m^2			2,555
Total Transport per person		2,628	
Total Transport per person per10 m^2 over 10 years			525.6
Total Kg CO_2 10m^2			7,525.6

In this calculation it is assumed that an old building is refurbished, making the amount of embodied energy consumed relatively low, even allowing for embodied energy. An assumption is made about the energy in use, which is considerably lower than that for an air-conditioned office building. This is open to debate but has been assumed for the purposes of illustration.

Concerning transport to and from the building, different assumptions have been made in terms of kilometres travelled per journey, and the percentage of days per year on which the distances are travelled. Although the converted apartments are assumed to be in a town or city centre, the assumption is that during evenings and weekends the individual will travel considerable distances, accumulating a large number of car kilometres per year.

The total transport cost per person is then calculated over a 10-year period per 10m^2. As with the air-conditioned office building, an estimate can be made for the use of this residential building over a 10-year period, assuming that each person occupies 50m^2.

These two examples provide the framework for similar calculation to allow calculation of the estimated total consumption of energy per person over time.

The following points should be noted.

- The figure related to energy is per 10 m^2 which for an office is one person but for a residential building is 20% of one person (using 50 m^2).
- There are major differences between new buildings and conversions because of the inherent embodied energy of the original structure.

Table 4.12: Energy and buildings per person use expressed in km CO_2 per 10 m² over 20 years

	Transport over 10 years	% relating to transport	Transport over 20 years	% relating to transport
Office Air-conditioned in-town	33792	11	37584	20
Office Air-conditioned out-of-town	36753	18	43473	31
Office Old Conversion in-town	14964	24	18564	31
Retail Shopping Centre out-of-town	25164	20	30274	34
Retail Park out-of-town	22588	29	29158	45
Retail Refurbishment in-town	17176	27	21739	34
Leisure New out-of-town	28329	36	38549	53
Leisure Old Refurbished in-town	12158	30	16168	37
Industrial Warehouse New	2769	48	4137	66
Industrial Production	13566	33	18126	10
Industrial Old Specialist	7566	60	12126	15
Institution New (School/Hospital)	21317	11	23507	19
Institution Old (Residential New House)	16989	11	18814	16
Residential New House	17520	3	18640	6
Residential New Apartment	14520	3.5	15040	7
Residential Old House	8925	7	9451	11
Residential Old Apartment/Conversion	7525	6	8051	13

- Transport to and from the building has a major impact on the total energy consumed, especially if the building is outside the town, and if a 20-year transport energy calculation is assumed. Out-of-town leisure buildings are very heavy users of transport energy.

The debate and illustrations above provide an insight into the complex nature of energy efficiency as it affects buildings in use. The combined effects of energy used, embodied and related to transport is not readily calculable because of the number of simplifying assumptions that are necessary within the process; however there is a clear demonstration that energy is or should be a major issue. It is important to reduce the use in a building of energy from non-renewable sources and that which increases pollution in its production. The growing use of renewable sources and the consideration of the use of other forms of energy may change the emphasis on this topic in the future and place greater emphasis on some of the following issues.

Materials, products and environmental sustainability

The selection of appropriate materials for a building has wide-ranging consequences in terms of its initial impact on the environment; however more relevant to the theme of this guide is the relationship between materials, products and their maintenance and potential re-use. At its simplest a building which is made from low-maintenance and re-usable materials is inherently more sustainable than one that is not.

Durability might be considered to be an obvious prerequisite for a sustainable building; indeed this was one of the clearest findings from the survey conducted as part of the *Buildings: a new life* project. A building that lacks the physical capacity to survive is not truly sustainable but Pratt (1991) noted that surprisingly some modern materials were of such limited durability that they failed even before the building went into service. This he attributed to a lack of understanding of the behaviour of materials and buildings.

There is a link between the choice of materials today and the future sustainability of buildings. Some materials require a significantly different energy and CO_2 production in their manufacture than others. For example in a low rise building of traditional construction concrete, plasterboard, bricks and mortar represent about 75% of the total embedded energy. The aim within both new design

---

Box 4.2 Materials and embodied energy

The origin of the materials or products used can have a major effect on the embodied energy in the building. For the UK market, high-performance wooden windows from Sweden have a high transport energy component as do Danish boilers designed to make use of waste products such as domestic refuse.

Before the advent of rail transport in the 19th century and later the development of road transport, the movement of building materials was limited to within about ten miles unless there was easy access to water (either the sea or inland waterways) when considerably greater distances could be contemplated.

This gave rise to very location-specific forms of vernacular architecture which now have a social and cultural value and interest. Consideration of the use of locally produced materials would have similar benefits today in both social and environmental sustainability.

Millennium Village, Greenwich, London
Reducing embodied energy.

- Impact on the global environment through CO_2 and other emissions;
- Impact on the local community through quarrying, felling or transport;
- Impact of the production processes;
- Embodied energy content;
- Health hazards involved in manufacture, installation, maintenance or demolition.

There is a strong link between environmental responsibility and the choice of building materials. While at first sight the relevance of this to the decision as to redevelop or refurbish might seem academic there are a number of reasons why it is not:

- The choice of materials used for renewal or refurbishment will influence comparative costs right across the triple bottom line;
- Some materials give rise to high maintenance demands which affect future economic and environmental factors;
- The reusability and ability to recycle some materials is an important consideration. A building that is capable of being recycled in terms of its materials involves fewer environmental consequences in its loss than one where demolition would lead to waste only.

and refurbishment projects should be towards reducing embodied energy through the selection of appropriate materials such as timber framing as opposed to heavy masonry construction.

In the selection of materials the following principles should be taken into account based on research by Monteith (1973).

Renewables

Wherever possible materials from renewable sources should be used since they will not deplete global resources and generally are CO_2 neutral. In principle timber and other crops are renewable sources but the over-use of some materials such as hardwoods from the tropical rain forests not only removes material faster than it is replaced but also gives rise to fundamental changes in the ecology, making areas barren for decades to come. For instance the effects of intensive sheep farming in East Anglia in the middle ages can still be seen and the overcropping of woodland in China created a fuel shortage which lasted from 1400 to 1800 giving rise to a bamboo-based technology. Organisations like CARM (Centre for Advanced & Renewable Materials) support research into new materials such as the environmentally sustainable, carbon-neutral insulating material produced from locally grown flax and hemp fibres (www.carmtechnology.co.uk).

Prefabrication

Prefabrication is not a perfect solution. Offering substantial benefits in the control of on-site waste, better quality control, improved control of air permeability and faster construction times it would appear to be so, but against that must be set the need to have a sufficient market to establish construction lines, leading to national or even international distribution networks with the associated transport costs. Large elements can cause congestion on roads, increasing the travel time and energy consumption of others.

The major problem with prefabrication may arise in longer term maintenance since this can involve specialist products or operatives which deny the economic benefits to the local community, and in other cases regular maintenance work may require gaskets or other items to be extruded to specifications to suit the original profiles. For instance the Lustron House (1) was designed as a prefabricated, adaptable housing system but required a maintenance engineer to visit in order to carry out alterations and maintenance while the White Tower roadside catering chain developed a demountable fast food offer to meet the changing needs of the early American road networks which allowed the company to minimise their costs in moving to meet new markets, but denied the local building trade valuable work and also left abandoned sites behind. To some degree these disadvantages have been minimised by an approach which places the prefabrication plant on site which is used for housing on the Greenwich

Peninsula where it is claimed to deliver a 28% saving in time as well as less road congestion and a more responsive system if errors are found on site (Horton and Arnold, 2003).

The use of recyclable materials

Significant amounts of materials are used in construction every year, such as six tonnes of aggregate and two tonnes of concrete (half of it reinforced with metal bars) per head of the population. Many of these materials are lost to reclamation but some are capable of being recycled.

The findings of the *Buildings: a new life* project demonstrated that the prevailing view was that the capacity of the building materials to be re-cycled was not a strong influence on building longevity. Although some materials can be re-used, the cost balanced against the environmental benefit that might accrue is not governing the decision-making process. If energy costs increase or as sustainability awareness grows there is an expectation that the capacity to re-cycle materials could become more important. An understanding of the capacity of the materials used for re-cycling is therefore important in considering sustainable construction.

Table 4.13: Comparative UK energy requirements

Materials	GJ/Tonne
Aluminium	270
Polyethylene	100
Polyvinyl chloride	80
Copper	50
Steel	35
Glass	20
Cement	6
Timber	4
Clay bricks	4
Cement	3
Aerated concrete	2
Concrete	1.5

Source: Taylor (2000)

A selection of typical materials that may be encountered in appraisal of existing buildings is considered below in Box 4.3 to identify the kind of issues which can arise in their selection.

Box 4.3 Recycling of materials

Wood: Wood is one of the easiest materials to recycle and making use of old timbers for new purposes is largely dictated by the economics of selection and of cleaning up for reuse. Ultimately the final material can still be used as an energy source, but there are committed recycling experts who are concerned about the potential toxicity of some of the preservation treatments. Use of smaller timber sections for laminated work can be useful in providing large structural elements from what might otherwise be waste material, and similarly wood chip can be used to form slabs and boards to maximise the use of the material.

Aluminium: Although a high energy user in original extraction, aluminium has the advantage of being relatively easily recycled and formed into new products. As a result commercial aluminium contains about 30% recycled material with an embodied energy content of about a quarter that of primary aluminium.

Plastics: An increasing range of plastics can be recycled, particularly those based on thermo-plastics. Even thermo-setting materials can be ground up to form an 'aggregate' for new materials and the Plaky table or the Seaweed Chair from the 1995 Mutant Materials exhibition at the Museum of Modern Art in New York are good examples of this.

Clay products: Bricks, faïence blocks and some tiles can be recovered from a building especially where they are bedded in a weak mortar. Whole elements can often command a sufficient premium as architectural salvage to make reclamation viable and to help pay for demolition costs. Poorer materials if clean can be crushed and used for hardcore. Consideration for the future demolition of the building and the ease with which the individual components can be recovered could significantly assist in their recyclability.

Concrete: Where there is a substantial requirement for fill or general hardcore the use of clean crushed concrete from the demolition of a previous building can be an economically viable alternative to removal from site and provides a degree of recycling.

Glass: Glass is a recyclable material and one which contributes to energy conservation both by reducing the need for artificial light and by the energy gain which can be harnessed to provide heating on a south facing facade (the energy required for manufacture is recovered by passive gain in about one week in October). The prospects for 'intelligent' glass which can react to environmental conditions make this material both interesting and promising but it must be borne in mind that inappropriate use can give rise to heat and consequently energy losses and gains which conflict with the efficient running of the building. Many glasses are imported with consequent high transport costs and the recovery of broken or redundant glass from buildings is rare, reducing this material's potential for reuse.

There is difficulty in predicting future uses for redundant goods – car tyres are a good example. In Westley, California there is the largest dump of tyres in the world, estimated at over 38 million. They have considerable implications for pollution but uses are now being found for the material. Twenty percent of asphalt laid in road construction in America has to contain rubber from tyres, one mile of road uses 16,000 tyres and it is claimed produces a surface which lasts twice as long, a double benefit. Tyres are also now being vaporised at 450°F at which temperature light oil and methane can be produced (Papanek, 1995).

The form of construction may dictate the degree to which materials can be recycled and this in turn should influence the decision as to whether to refurbish or redevelop. If materials cannot be recycled then they add to the waste problem in the event of demolition but if demolition does not lead to a total loss of the material and they can be recycled in environmentally and economically acceptable ways, this could influence the decision towards redevelopment. Composite materials or prefabricated panels often mean that the cost of separating the component parts makes it uneconomic and it may also prevent upgrading of insulation or other parts of the construction to meet new standards and legislation, an important consideration in the light of the EU Directive requirements to re-license public buildings at frequent intervals.

Table 4.14: The re-usability of materials

Material	Recycling
Coated steels	60–70% of steel is recycled but due to demand the proportion of recycled steel to the total used is around 25%.
Aluminium	95% of aluminium used in buildings is recycled but due to the demand for the material the proportion of recycled material t total demand is around 60%. Life span in excess of 40 years.
Copper	55% of copper used in buildings is recycled. Life span in excess of 100 years.
Lead	Very recyclable and high scrap value. Life span in excess of 100 years.
Zinc	Europe recycles 90% of zinc roofing. Life span 80–100 years.
Clay	Good potential for reuse and afterwards can be used as aggregate. Life span 30–100 years.
Slate	Good reuse potential. Life span in the order of 100 years.
Concrete	Could be reused but more often they are recycled as fill. Life span 30–100 years.
Timber shingles	Tend to degrade and therefore cannot be reused. Waste material might be suitable as a fuel but preservatives may present a problem. Life span 20–50 years.
Felts and asphalt	Can generally be recycled but there is little recycled roofing in the UK at present. Life span 50 years.
Membranes	Single ply roofing can usually be recycled and mechanically fixed EPDM systems are very durable and can often be reused. Life span 20–50 years.

Source: *Ecotech* Issue 7 May 2003

To summarise, the potential re-usability of materials should be taken into account in order to minimise embodied energy and to reduce waste as part of the decision to re-use or demolish a building and to satisfy the requirements of environmental sustainability. From the research, it would appear to be a factor that is seldom seen as other than an economic consideration.

Building Maintenance as a factor of environmental sustainability

The durability and maintenance of buildings is of primary concern in promoting building sustainability and in turn is linked to the choice and use of materials. For example, if a material used is difficult to maintain, the life span of both the component and potentially the building will be compromised.

The ambition behind much of the research carried out by BRE and others into environmental sustainability is linked to life-cycle costing which in turn depends considerably on the maintenance regime adopted. Some materials imply a low quality and a tolerance of defects (for example, granolithic flooring) while others imply high quality regular cleaning and maintenance (marble floors by contrast). Similarly traditional cladding materials were generally intended to weather naturally, developing and enhancing their mouldings and surface texture over many years, whereas modern materials are often intended to undergo regular and frequent maintenance. Current building design reinforces this.

On the positive side, maintenance potentially provides a useful source of local employment, reducing travel and related energy consumption, but the negative aspect is that if the technology of the building and the materials used are reliant on specialist components or expertise, then this benefit will be frustrated. For example, the prismatic glass used at the Lloyds building in the City of London is manufactured in Germany using rollers owned by Lloyds and requiring a minimum run of 12 tons of material at any one time. This material has to be stored until it is required so, while the material itself may provide an excellent performance, its replacement does not comply with sustainability criteria. This demonstrates the complexity in trying to arrive at environmentally sustainable solutions when choosing materials.

Water conservation

The use of water has two major effects on environmental sustainability. Its inefficient use

Table 4.15: The pollution effects of building materials

Material	Pollution
Coated steels	The emission of dioxins during the production of iron is controlled in the UK by legal limits. Recycling may release further dioxins when coatings such as PVC are incinerated although some sheet materials use coatings which can be recycled without this risk. Stainless steel production involves the release of toxic metals and the use of heavy metals in the alloy.
Aluminium	There is a possible risk of the release of dioxins from machine oils during secondary aluminium smelting, but the main cause for concern is the loss of tropical forest during strip mining. Figures released by the Aluminium Federation indicate 70% of land is now returned to native forest.
Copper	Concerns have been expressed regarding the consequences of copper mining and the detrimental effects of copper in rainwater run off from copper roofs both of which are contested.
Lead	Lead can be highly toxic and may pose problems during mining and processing while rainwater run off may result in water contamination.
Zinc	Historically mining and processing waste has been associated with environmental problems but emissions are thought to have been in decline since the 1970s. Both high and low levels of zinc can be detrimental to human beings.
Clay	Emissions during manufacture can include chlorine compounds but generally there are few toxicity issues.
Slate	No pollution problems other than the effects of quarrying on the landscape.
Concrete	Portland cement can release toxins on firing and acrylic paint used to control efflorescence may contain acrylonitrile which is a suspected carcinogen.
Timber shingles	The basic material has no toxicity issues but the fireproofing and preservation treatments can be toxic.
Felts and asphalt	The majority of asphalt is made up of limestone fillers and aggregate with no toxicity issues. The bitumen represents only 12% of roofing grade material.
Membranes	There is considerable debate about the effects of materials such as PVC used in some membranes with parties taking strongly opposing positions.
Green roofs	These roofs can actually reduce pollution by capturing carbon dioxide and increasing oxygen levels. In addition vegetation can reduce air dust and traffic particulates.

Source: Ecotech (2003)

to meet new needs it will not survive. An eighteenth century, five-storey town house needed servants to carry the coal, bring hot water and run the household and a Victorian warehouse no longer fulfils the sophisticated needs of a modern materials handling system. Both have had to be adapted in order to survive.

Some buildings are more easily adapted than others and a few are even designed to change as an integral part of their conception and continued existence. Brand (1997) argues that buildings '*learn and evolve*' in order to survive; commercial premises he claims often do this kaleidoscopically while domestic buildings have a steadier rate of change. Brand states that there is a design

imperative and that an adaptable building has to allow slippage between the differently-paced systems of Site, Structure, Skin, Services, Space Plan and Stuff (furniture and fittings)'. Predicting change is difficult and Brand suggests that in organisations and in buildings evolution is always, and indeed necessarily, surprising!

Recognition that buildings cannot continue to fulfil their original uses indefinitely was contained in a debate at the LSE in the 1930s when it was declared that commercial buildings should have a life of no more than forty years. At that time of modernist ideas, environmental issues had not entered into the debate but in an austere post World War II environment, Hartland Thomas

(1947) declared that '*the rapidity with which buildings become obsolete long before they wear out makes the question of designing buildings with a view to subsequent alterations one of the major architectural problems of the day.*'

Adaptability is not restricted to the ability to alter the building configuration to meet new needs and processes, but also concerns upgrading the building to meet new servicing demands or to reflect changing building standards by increasing thermal performance or other environmental criteria. This ability to adapt was investigated in the *Buildings: a new life* research project and the perceptions of most building stakeholders was that adaptability was one of the key factors that determined building life. When this was followed through with case studies, the same finding emerged. A building whose form allowed change, particularly across use type was found to be more likely to survive through all points in the economic cycle.

The correlation between the adaptability and sustainability of a building is leading commercial buildings to focus on issues such as flexibility with large floor plates allowing for varying use patterns. The perception persists however in some areas that there is a standard life expectancy of office buildings. While *Buildings: a new life* has shed some further light on the relationship between a building's life and its adaptability, more work is required to understand more about the design qualities required to give long term adaptability. Adaptability has certainly been shown to be one of the characteristics of a sustainable building (see for example, Sayce and Ellison, 2003).

Demolition

Demolition and sustainability may seem to be contradictory but there can be good reasons for designing a new building for a short life if it is to meet a particular need or location. In other cases a comparison may be needed between the demolition of an existing structure and its replacement with a new building rather than its retention and revitalisation. All materials wear out in time and need replacement, at which point it is necessary to consider whether replacement/repair, complete demolition or the replacement of major elements only is the most suitable method. Insulation is a

relatively new concept and may not have the same life as the building, or it may deteriorate over time if it is embedded, in which case the question arises as to whether it is practical to renew it, as has occurred within the well-publicised problems with insulation in cavity brick walls or in cladding panels (see, for example, Webb, 2002).

Also associated with the issue of demolition are the factors already discussed under re-use of materials waste management and pollution. Inevitably demolition has implications in relation to all these criteria of environmental sustainability.

Biodiversity

It is increasingly clear that there is a need to protect and positively encourage a diverse range of animal and plant life. Sometimes even common species are under threat and the grounds of a building can provide the opportunity to encourage appropriate species within a suitable habitat.

Individual buildings are unlikely to have a direct effect on biodiversity except where they are part of a larger scheme set in parkland or a landscaped setting but as mentioned above, where they are the cause of light or other pollution effect they can have significant biodiversity implications and this is an areas in which there are potential taxation liabilities as measures are taken to further environmental protection.

Accessibility

The link between accessibility and economic sustainability is clear as it is important for the economic functioning of a building with a need for goods, staff and customers to gain access easily and conveniently. The connection with environmental sustainability is less obvious but it exists nonetheless. The location and availability of public transport as well as accommodation for private transport such as cars and cycles and possibly in the future smaller motorised scooters, as well as sound access for goods vehicles will be of considerable importance in the attractiveness and thus sustainability of a building. Inside the building rapid access by stair, lift or escalator will be important. If the building does not succeed in these areas, it will ultimately fail.

Over recent years there has also been a growing

concern to ensure that everyone has equal access to the property including those with impaired mobility and those with sight or hearing disabilities. Inside the building they need similar facilities in the form of lavatories and suitable provision for means of escape in the event of fire or other disaster. In historic buildings making provision for those with poor sight can have a significant effect on the cultural environmental qualities of the interior.

Retrofitting such facilities can be very costly and in the case of small buildings prohibitive in the effect on useable space. Relaxations of legislation are available but in the longer term consideration of the level of provision needed will need to be balanced with the social implications of unequal accessibility.

Summary

The discussion of environmental sustainability outlined at the beginning of this chapter demonstrates that, while matters of energy use are very important, they are certainly not the only environmental factors that will influence building life and building sustainability. In terms of energy it is clear that the embedded energy required to form a building cannot be ignored and the failure to do so can lead to incorrect conclusions for sustainability. When the energy related to access is included, the overall location and accessibility factors take on considerable importance to environmental sustainability.

The nature of the materials used including their re-usability potential are also important considerations in determining the environmental sustainability of a building, as are matters of pollution and waste management. It is across a range of these issues that building can become increasingly at risk from the effects of new legislation and fiscal controls.

Arising from the discussions within the chapter and the *Buildings: a new life* project are a number of key questions that should form the minimum agenda for the Building Sustainability Assessment Tool provided in Chapter 6. It is emphasised that these need to be augmented and adapted according to individual circumstances.

- Does the building meet current and likely future imposed environmental standards, both internally and externally?
- Is the building efficient in terms of energy usage, or could it be made so?
- In terms of embodied energy, what are the implications for lengthening building life through judicious refurbishment as opposed to redevelopment?
- Does the building contain or emit noxious or pollutant materials and what are the implications for these in the event of redevelopment?
- What are the environmental implications of its location for its current or proposed use, including the energy implications of travel to the building?
- Does the building give rise to any ecological considerations in terms of its use (such as energy) or materials?
- Is the building adaptable such that it provides an internal environment that meets the current needs of occupiers and the needs of future occupiers?

Many of the environmental issues are capable of measurement. This has encouraged a narrow focus on such matters as a means of establishing sustainability but not only does this potentially ignore the other issues of the triple bottom line but can distort the findings even within the confines of environmental issues. It is of great importance that the conflicts are recognised, that the quick fix is not the adopted solution but that a complete and balanced picture is sought through means such as the BSAT described in Chapter 6.

Endnote

1   Jester TC, Porcelain Enamel (1995) ed Jester T, *Twentieth Century Materials*, McGrawHill.

Chapter 5

Social Sustainability of Buildings

Principal Messages:

- *There is no single definition of social sustainability; it depends on the context.*
- *Principal concerns of social sustainability include issues of health and safety, well-being and respect for people.*
- *Social sustainability is increasingly related to matters of corporate governance and business ethics; collectively labelled as Corporate Social Responsibility (CSR).*
- *Economic success is now seen as linked to adherence to Corporate Social Responsibility (CSR) principles.*
- *For buildings, social sustainability relates to matters of location, planning and building regulations.*

A definition of social sustainability

Social sustainability is not easy to define. In the workplace it relates primarily to issues of:

- health and well-being, including health and safety and the relevant regulations;
- employment including utilisation of skills and knowledge;
- eradication of poverty and child labour;
- inclusivity, equity and co-operation;
- relationships, working and personal and including respect for people and stakeholder dialogues;
- information management and security;
- values, norms and ethics;
- fair governance.

These issues are about dealing with people fairly in the cause of promoting what UK government has espoused as a better quality of life (DETR, 1999) which through the application of Agenda 21 to the policies at local level aims to create equitable and sustainable communities.

The Natural Step organisation (www.natural step.org) in defining its principles of sustainability

describes the aims thus:

contribute as much as we can to the goal of meeting human needs in our society and world-wide, going over and above all the substitution and dematerialization measures taken in meeting the first three objectives of sustainability. (1)

The message they promote is of the efficient use of resources within a framework of fairness and proper responsibility so that the needs of all people can be best assured now and on an inter-generational basis.

At first sight, this principle appears to be incontestable but in reality it is more complex. At a macro-level, the combined efforts of the United Nations (UN) and the International Labour Organisation (ILO) have found it difficult to move beyond the rhetoric into substantive action. To take an example: while many in the developed world may think it socially unacceptable to exploit child labour and seek to outlaw or to regulate it strictly, to countries in the developing world it may represent the opportunity to gain economic advantage.

Accordingly, to agree on the implementation and definition of actions that should be taken in order to achieve the principles of a 'fairer' society are both difficult and contentious. The World Summit in Johannesburg in 2002 did not succeed in moving forward on an agreement for substantive progress on sustainability in terms of social policy. Instead the shift is towards implementation and enforcement of previously agreed principles.

Social sustainability: a matter of process and regulation

The difficulties inherent in defining and implementing social sustainability are debated in the research papers of the Sigma Project (Henriques and Raynard, 2001). The authors define social sustainability in terms of both process and substantive achievement elements. Noting the difficulties experienced at the macro and governmental level they advocate a process definition where social sustainability needs to be seen in terms of adherence to standards, the development of which will set the frameworks and mechanisms within which the goals can be set and measured.

It follows from this that an essential ingredient of social sustainability is governance and both self and governmental regulation.

Fair governance and Corporate Social Responsibility

The concepts of Corporate Social Responsibility (CSR) and Socially Responsible Investment (SRI) are rooted in the Quaker Movement (HSBC, 2002) but more recently have found expression in movements like the boycott of South African goods in opposition to apartheid. What is new is the manner in which companies are increasingly embracing the principles. The screening approach of excluding investment is being replaced by engagement and advocacy between investors and government over social concerns. Corporate reporting now places an increasing obligation on companies to make their policies explicit in terms of Corporate Social Responsibility which in turn is leading to the perception that strong implementation of fair policies may lead to increased competitive advantage. This case was made strongly by the Sustainable Construction

Task Force (2001) who argued that a lack of attention to sustainability, including Corporate Social Responsibility, is likely to result in a decreased reputation and increased risk to profitability.

Human well-being

There are several strands to human well-being ranging from issues such as the quality of the environment within which people operate to matters of physical protection and security. On a global scale it embraces the right to self-determination and political freedom; on a micro scale it encompasses the right to live without fear of attack in safe city streets.

Another important aspect of human well-being is that of health and education. Indeed these dominate the human development indicators published by the United Nations Development Programme (www.hdr.undp.org) which lists the indicators of human well-being as follows:

- Life expectancy, including both at birth and overall. This is a surrogate for health;
- Education, including participation rates at both secondary and tertiary levels and adult literacy;
- Gross Domestic Product (GDP) per head.

While the composition of the index is not without its critics it does demonstrate the emphasis placed on health and education as measures of well-being.

Worker issues

Worker issues are closely linked to human well-being. They concern fair remuneration as well as health and safety in the workplace, working hours etc. With global trade, the issue of worker protection from exploitation is not a domestic matter only. As Klein (2000) illustrated clearly, the issue of worker exploitation in for example the Far East is a matter of relevance to US or UK based companies who import goods and services.

Government response: towards a better quality of life: indicators of progress

The UK government's response to social sustainability is embodied within its policy documents (www.sustainable-development.gov.uk) using indicators that encompass:

- Output
- Investment
- Employment
- Poverty and social exclusion
- Education
- Health
- Housing
- Crime
- Climate change
- Air quality
- Road traffic
- River water strategy
- Wildlife
- Land use
- Waste

It seeks to measure on a year-by-year basis the way in which government initiatives are leading to progress in these areas. From a built environment perspective, some indicators such as housing, climate change and road traffic have clear implications while measures such as crime also relate to building design and layout and waste to both the impact of design on waste disposal and to the construction industry is one of the key producers of waste during the building process.

Accounting for social sustainability

The early development of the sustainability agenda was strongly linked to that of environmentalism. It is only much more recently that social issues have been added to this and the economic issues to create the triple bottom line. It follows that matters of accounting for social sustainability are also of recent origin. The Association of Chartered Certified Accountants (www.acca.co.uk) has for example made awards to companies in connection with the quality of their environmental accounting since 1991, but for social accounting only since 1999 and for full sustainability accounting since 2001.

Another manifestation of the role of social responsibility within the accounting process is the development of both the Dow Jones Sustainability Index and the FTSE4Good Index. Companies without sound social accounting procedures to implement related policies are unlikely to meet the criteria for inclusion within these indices.

The development of social accountability has led to a range of initiatives from the well-known Investors in People to AA1000 which requires organisations seeking the standard to demonstrate how social sustainability is not only accounted for but embedded within an organisation.

Social sustainability: from macro to micro concerns

The definition of social sustainability given above and the issues it raises can be viewed very much as macro concerns for policy makers at town, national and international level. They are focused on people concerns and the actual level of the *building* is not really addressed. It is the clustering of buildings into a specified identified 'place' that has primarily attracted the policy makers.

At a micro-level, social sustainability has been increasingly identified as synonymous with the drive for CSR. This is no longer an option in many cases, with financial institutions now obliged to have CSR policies and many other organisations seeing it as a matter of risk reduction and competitive advantage (Sustainable Construction Focus Group 2001).

Here the focus is on policy. The implementation at the level of individual decision-making is more problematic, for example investors with their commitment to CSR can track their share performance through FTSE4Good but they are not yet able to track their property investments in a similar way as no appraisal tool exists yet, although one is being developed (Sayce and Ellison, 2003 [a] and [b]).

Social sustainability of buildings

If the goal is towards more sustainable buildings, then the social sustainability characteristics of buildings should be considered as part of the evaluation as being worthy of retention. At the level of the building, social sustainability may be a goal but it is not yet one that has been reached in any quantifiable way. This section and the BSAT (Building Sustainability Assessment Tool) aim to address this deficiency, at least in part.

In order to investigate the issue of social sustainability of buildings it must be seen from the perspective of both an internal and external

---

Box 5.1: The growing commitment to SCR

Below are some statements that indicate the growing commitment to matters of social sustainability within the property and construction industry stakeholder.

Land Securities in their company accounts state:
We are developing a Group-wide system for managing our CSR activities.....and in future we will aim to report on CSR to include our environmental report, every year.... Our continued inclusion in the FTSE4Good index as well as our leadership position in the DJSI, where in 2002 we were named European Real Estate Market Leader, demonstrates our commitment to CSR (www.investis.com/reports/ls_ar_2003/)

Amec too is committed to social sustainability
AMEC is committed to building a sustainable business based upon the achievement of a positive balance of economic, environmental and social benefits and to continuous improvement and regular public reporting on our performance AMEC's sustainability programme is founded on the indicators of performance based on our guiding principles.

These are quoted (www.amec.com) as based on responsibilities to customers, shareholders, health and safety, the environment, cultural diversity, ethical practice and community support.

Morley Fund Managers, who have set up Igloo – the specialist urban regeneration fund, state in their report:
we believe we have a responsibility to encourage best practice in environmental management, employment practices, human rights, community relations and products or services. Our SRI engagement strategy, initiated in February 2001 applies across all Morley's funds and has been put in place because we believe that these issues are relevant to a company's performance and ultimately share price performance. Our engagement strategy has enabled us to better identify and address CSR issues within our own organisation. We have also been able to encourage companies in both our SRI and non-SRI funds to address CSR issues in order to better manage business risk and protect shareholder value.
(www.cgnu.co.uk/responsibility/2002report/reports/business/morleyfund_management.htm)

These collectively provide a demonstration of the commitment across a range of property-related organisations to promote social responsibility.

---

stakeholder. The difficulty is that it is not possible to base such as analysis on quantitative data as is largely possible in relation to the economic perspective. How can the potential of a building to contribute to its external stakeholders' well-being be evaluated?

During the *Buildings: a new life* project, investigations pointed to the importance of social factors to the possible continued life of a building (see Appendix A for the summary of survey findings). Indeed the survey pointed to social factors (including legal, location and likeability) as of far greater importance in the building decision-making process than environmental concerns.

The project highlighted that very few studies had measured the efficiency of a building in terms of its social working environment with reference to the function of the building for business, the capacity of the space to meet occupiers' needs, and the changing nature of such measurements as organisations changed over time.

Where such studies had taken place it was revealed that they tended to be either private domain surveys carried out for individual organisations and therefore not published, or post-occupancy evaluations of new buildings that have been designed with sustainability criteria in mind, not *post-hoc* studies of older buildings.

The *Buildings: a new life* project, through a series of debates, questionnaires and case studies has revealed that a number of social issues are critical in terms of determining whether or not a building would be retained or demolished. Indeed, one of the main findings of the project was that social factors, including legal and management issues are often more critical that either environmental or economic considerations.

This finding is extremely important as it has enormous implications for the design of new buildings and the setting up of their initial leases. It also has implications for the way in which a building may be managed over time. In terms of critical decision-making in relation to an existing building, the decision whether or not to retain should include this social dimension.

Likeability and lovability: the building's appeal

The external stakeholder perspective

Sometimes social sustainability can result in longevity due to positive external stakeholder concerns. A building under risk is capable of producing a public reaction in support of its survival despite having little economic value, it is simply liked enough by external stakeholders to influence the decision. This impact, that of public perception and reaction (the so-called 'loveability' factor) is difficult to quantify. Yet the fact that it exists is undeniable.

Deriving lessons about sustainability from polls such as this is difficult; buildings that were both modern (Stanstead Airport and the Eden Project) and old produced high degrees of respect and love, so age was not the issue. Undoubtedly more research is required into what does create a building that external stakeholders deem loveable and so worthy of retention. Building quality and the ability to provide a sense of locus may be indicators, but even that is not proven. There is an emotional response here and also a question of association with events and people. This is of course reflected in the criteria for listing, whereas simple public liking is not.

The internal stakeholder

To the internal stakeholders likeability and emotional response are different. The measure to which a building is liked by its occupiers can be assessed through satisfaction surveys for which numerous templates exist. For likeability there is a distinct link with matters of functionality. A building that does not 'perform' functionally and in which for example services are inefficient and focused on the needs of the occupier are not likely to be well liked. Other factors come in to play here: the internal configuration may or may not be an impediment to social inter-actions. It is here that small floor plate high rise buildings score badly, as vertical circulation will always be more difficult to achieve than horizontal. If a building is to be liked, it should be adaptable to a configuration that will allow people to circulate freely and benefit from informal social interaction. Other factors, such as aesthetics and the sense of purpose and 'being' can affect the reactions of those entering it on a daily basis.

Rodboro Buildings, Guildford
These buildings, originally used as a car factory for DenNis Cars was listed without an economic use, was threatened with demolition and remained empty for many years. The building caught the public imagination and has been adapted and successfully used as a public house for JD Weatherspoons and for a music academy on the upper floors.

Tricorn Centre, Portsmouth
Constructed in the 1960s and effectively abandoned less than 30 years later, the centre remains an eyesore in the middle of Portsmouth. The nature of the commercial space and the threatening qualities of the public realm combined with a questionable location have rendered the shopping centre unsustainable. Additionally accessibility proved problematic. The Tricorn has however proved too flexible for adaption and uneconomic to develop.

Box 5.2: What makes a building loved?

In 2001 the BBC ran a poll of Britain's most loved and most hated buildings. (2) The eventual winner was Durham Cathedral which was widely regarded as producing an uplifting emotion, with the derelict Tricorn Shopping Centre in Portsmouth being voted the most hated building. Interestingly, the National Theatre on the South Bank while being ranked fourth as the most loved also featured on the most hated short list.

In terms of retail space the views of internal and external stakeholders may merge far more than with offices, as the shopper enters the building and gains a shared experience.

A sense of place and locality

In terms of social sustainability the agenda will relate not just to the actual building but to the environment in which it is placed. A building that is out of context with its environment is less likely to survive over time than one that is by itself capable of creating a sense of place and so will draw economic vitality back to an area. To this extent the role of older buildings within regeneration schemes can be critical.

If a building is likely to score highly on the likeability/loveability criteria it may be that it has the characteristics that will lead to successful revitalisation of an area. For example, the characteristics of the Floral Hall at Covent Garden were well-known by literary association and this may have been a key factor in the undoubted success of the rescue scheme, which in turn led to increased values and economic success of the area. Conversely, the re-use of London's County Hall, despite its also being a landmark building did not have the same dynamic effect and it was only with the construction of the London Eye that the revival of place occurred.

Listing: a measure of external value?

It can be observed that buildings retained by society and 'listed' as being of historical or architectural interest tend to be 'wealth consuming' buildings (see Chapter 3). These 'listed' structures are rarely considered to be efficient 'wealth

Hoover Building, Great West Road, London
A measure of the external value of a building, the former Hoover Vacuum Cleaner Factory almost suffered the fate of the nearby Firestone Factory which was demolished on the eve of listing. However the building has been retained and substantially converted to provide a Tesco food store

creating' buildings meeting the modern needs of manufacturing or office service industries.

The tendency to 'list' non-wealth creating buildings as being of special historic or architectural interest is a function of the early interests of the conservation movement. William Morris and his colleagues were mainly interested in protecting ecclesiastical buildings and early university and similar structures. However, the whole thrust of conservation widened the range of interests, with the Georgian Society in 1937 being set up in protest against a limited range of interests. More recently, many formerly wealth creating buildings have been listed. These range from 19th century factories and warehouses to Birds Eye offices at Walton on Thames, Peter Jones modern warehouse at Gunnells Wood in Hertfordshire, or the Hoover factory on the Great West Road, West London.

Financial considerations are specifically not

Birds Eye Building, Walton-on-Thames, Surrey
This complex was listed as part of the exemplars of modern office building at Grade II. The owners (Unilever) have entered into a management agreement to assist with their use of the office space without incurring the additional burdens of seeking listed building consent on every occasion. The community cultural issues of conservation are being addressed in a manner that minimises the conflicts with the occupiers' own sustainability agenda.

taken into account in listing, nor are external costs, for example environmental degradation or possibly economic stagnation. They are perhaps more a socio-cultural–political response to heritage.

English Heritage would argue that the time to take account of economic versus social issues is when an application comes in for modification work to be done. They adopt a similar attitude to all buildings, to energy conservation and even to means of escape. The problem is that there is no conformity in the decision making process with regard to balancing economic, environmental and social sustainability.

The internal stakeholder

When buildings are 'listed' for architectural or historical purposes there is almost always a private and/or social cost involved. Frequently the result is that the ability of the building to be adapted to meet changing occupier needs will be compromised and, by definition, the economic potential for redevelopment is significantly eroded (Scanlon *et al.*, 1994) Therefore, in the hands of the occupier and the owner, there may be a capital or rental loss and a possible decline in related productivity.

The current UK planning/listed building system takes no formal account of these wider costs to society. It is merely a political/emotional assess-ment of the structure, regardless of who pays for that decision. While there is clearly a difference between a listed or non listed building, the impact of a listing decision on the 'market value' of that building, and the wider 'social price' of that decision, are rarely quantified.

Despite this lack of data, a few studies have been undertaken. In 2002 English Heritage, with IPD and the RICS Foundation, looked at the investment performance of listed office buildings . They found that within the IPD dataset (which only represents 'investment' buildings) listed buildings can sometimes achieve higher returns than unlisted offices; however the returns generated by listed buildings tend to be more volatile than those of the unlisted buildings, leading to higher risk.

The main market value change occurs when the building is first listed, an issue that is not addressed when the decision to add to the 'list' is taken (Scanlon *et al.*, 1994).

From the viewpoint of the investor or owner-occupier therefore, there is a cost implicit in the listing process. To counter-balance this the listing process may add value for external stakeholders and this added value relates to the ambience and aesthetic provided by the building, its contribution to the sense of place and identity. It can therefore be important in defining the character of a location over time.

Adaptability

Brand (1997) identified a key factor that gave continuing life to buildings which was their ability to be adapted over time. To some extent this is a matter of function and form but it is more than this: both external and internal stakeholders will have changing requirements for buildings that relate to the social context.

The external stakeholder perspective

If it is to succeed over time any building must be capable of adaptation to meet changing social patterns. Some buildings are clearly more likely to succeed in this than others. As has been illustrated under economic sustainability, wealth consuming uses may be able to utilise a range of building forms but wealth creating uses may have more specific building requirements which is illustrated by the many redundant farm buildings which have been successfully given new lives as either residential units or as craft manufacturing and display spaces. Similarly food and drink outlets where the product on sale is first and foremost the ambience have often successfully utilised space that no longer meets the original user's needs. Many have now become instrumental in revitalising high streets where units are vacated by traditional retailers seeking larger stores to satisfy the needs of car borne shoppers

Successful re-use of a building is less likely where the building is complex in form (such as a shopping centre or multiplex cinema), although where a building has an emotional appeal and arouses vision and commitment almost anything is possible. For example, the widely acclaimed conversion of Bankside power station to the Tate Modern Gallery is an unexpected but extraordinarily appropriate re-use.

Bankside Power Station, London
At one time facing demolition, this
redundant power station, through its
conversion to the Tate Modern Art
Gallery, provided a powerful regeneration
impetus for this area of Southwark.

Internal stakeholder perspective

Over time, the standards required in order to fulfil
social aspirations and norms change. Such
changes may be manifest in changing requirements in relation to the specification and location
of buildings; for example, the late 20th century
witnessed significant changes in the way that
offices operate in terms of technology and working
practices.

These changes have been particularly manifest
in offices where demand has shifted from cellular
space and shallow floor plates, to open-plan deep
space which may not be compatible with older
buildings. For such occupiers the only acceptable
form to meet their operational needs may be by
new blocks which has implications for their location
since city centre sites may not be of sufficient
footprint to meet the occupational needs. The need
to accommodate the occupiers' requirements can
lead to construction in locations which have
environmental impacts in terms of transport (see
Chapter 4) and social implications in terms of lack
of complementary amenities for employees.

The changing needs of occupiers can lead to the
functional obsolescence of quite new buildings and
indeed this was the fate of many 1960s office
buildings whose rigid frames did not easily
accommodate the 1990s office requirements.
Relocation of their business occupiers can lead to
a complex sustainability issues. The new location
may have negative environmental and social

impacts, and the migration from small-scale
buildings that relate more easily to the human
dimension can potentially lead to a lack of vitality
within the areas they vacate, unless there is a
change in social habits that provides an alternative
set of occupiers. If this is missing then the whole
area may decline in terms of its social cohesion
and appeal and thus an internal decision based on
economic criteria can lead to both internal and
external stakeholders being adversely affected in
social terms.

For this reason, the ability to adapt to ensure
social continuance is regarded as a key factor in
assessing the social sustainability of a building.

The above discussion relates to office users and
indeed offices have been the chief subject of
studies on obsolescence (see for example,
Salway, 1985; Baum, 1991). With other building
types the issue is less well documented and may
or may not be less acute.

While office users and other wealth creating
activities tend to require purpose designed and
often modern space, the situation does not arise to
the same degree with wealth-consuming activities.
These may present different issues for adaptation.
The standard high street shop has for many years
been just that: a standard with a typical frontage of
6–8 metres and a preferred 20 m depth. Changes
in retailing systems however, and the necessity to
accommodate 'E-tailing' has led to a demand for
larger, more cost efficient, stores typically of two to
three times the capacity, and this has increased

the functional obsolescence of some town centre units.

Notwithstanding the great challenge in terms of flexibility within the high street, a greater problem may be faced by the owners of shopping centres where the original design is not conducive to the change that will accommodate the rising aspirations and changing shopping habits of consumers. Thus while many high street shops can still compete economically a hundred years after their original construction, some shopping centres lack the basic adaptability to withstand changing consumer patterns over much shorter time spans with the result that refurbishment cycles shorten.

The summary of issues concerning building adaptability thus leads to the key question in relation to the determination of a building's future.

Location

The commercial development community has held to the mantra of location, location, location as being fundamental to a successful development. But over time the quality of a location and indeed fashions, change so a building which was originally entirely appropriate may become obsolete in terms of location.

The *Buildings: a new life* study has led to the conclusion that a central location is more likely to survive where proximity to major public transport nodes exist. Indeed, with the Quality of Life indicators placing emphasis on matters such as air quality, traffic volumes, CO_2 emissions, an occupier who seeks to improve their CSR rating will be likely in the future to assess their locational requirements far more in terms of public transport than has been the case until recently.

Community uses have similar pressures and a building which is badly located will suffer by being unused, abused or just missed. Some forms of use will be more susceptible than others, discretionary uses such as leisure and most retailing have to be in the right location or, as at Bluewater, to create their location and sense of place.

Other uses such as housing are not funda-mentally so sensitive to transport issues but location will be equally affect their value.

Internal stakeholder perspective

The perceived quality of the area for a particular activity and the range of local amenities will be of interest to the occupiers and thus to the building owners. Again the point is made that it is the total context of location that is important and to a retailer this means access to customers as well as accessibility by suppliers. The matter of location is therefore inextricably linked to its future potential life. A building that is located with only a very small range of possible users is far less likely to be sustainable than one that has a location that is appropriate to a range of users.

There is a caveat to this however: buildings located in very high value areas and used for wealth-creation purposes may be vulnerable to change. In such cases, the economic value lies more in the site than the actual building and any possibility to extract a greater density of use may lead to redevelopment. Similarly, in such locations, the demand from users may be for highest quality internal environments and this again can test a building's adaptability to the limit or beyond.

External stakeholders

For the community the question is a matter of the degree to which the building and its users contribute to the quality of the local environment. The survey findings pointed to the quality of the environment as being of importance. For example, while building occupiers and owners did not see a strong connection between the desirability of a location in terms of such things as conservation status and the potential of a building to survive, this was considered very important to external stakeholders.

Legislation

The role of legislation in terms of building sustainability is two-fold. First it concerns the raft of construction legislation, including planning and building regulations. Second it concerns occupation legislation that affects the way a building may be utilised and managed. The occupation legislation covers aspects such as accessibility, health and safety and CSR.

London Wall, City of London
The development of this bombed area of London and its further redevelopment at the end of the last century provide clear evidence of the changing needs of wealth-creating buildings and their users.

Box 5.3: The changing needs of wealth-creating buildings

Offices in London Wall in the City of London, constructed in the 1960s, proved susceptible to early economic obsolescence and were redeveloped in under half their original design life. This raises the issue that, if 'future-proofing' is so difficult, should we build to last or are temporary structures more practical, using minimal recyclable materials and replacing them frequently?

Internal stakeholders

The building owner and occupier will obviously be affected in their decision-making by the constraints on the use, alteration or development of a particular building under the planning and planning regulation legislation. Key points that may influence the sustainability of the building will include the social legislation such as the Disability Discrimination Act which requires building owners to make 'reasonable' adaptation of their buildings by 2004.

Arguably for most commercial buildings, the matter of energy usage is one for the occupier, not the owner; however the recent and proposed changes to part L of the Building Regulations makes this of more direct interest to the party responsible for the shell of the building. With moves

Box 5.4: Changing policies: changing actions

Changing legislation and government policies may drive investing owners towards retention of their building stock or towards the acquisition of 'green' buildings.

The Igloo Urban Regeneration Fund has been created by Morley Fund Managers investing exclusively in urban regeneration projects. The Fund has strong socially responsible investment (SRI) characteristics and is aimed at attracting investors who are seeking to promote their CSR profiles. Other leading investors are now seeking to develop SRI policies towards property (Sayce and Ellison 2003 [a] and [b]).

Swiss Reinsurance Building, City of London

The Swiss Reinsurance building in London's St Mary's Axe, designed by Sir Norman Foster, has been heralded as both green and lean and may herald a greater awareness of and demand for eco-friendly buildings, based on CRS principles as well as economic returns.

Architect: Norman Foster

towards shorter leases consequent both on market practices and the introduction of a revised Commercial Lease code in 2002, the investing owner will need to become more actively involved with the building, regardless of their own CSR stance.

External stakeholders

From the external perspective, planning legislation and building regulation are both important means of protecting the community's interests. This can occur through Building Regulations control over structural stability or energy consumption or by planning control over incompatible uses or overload of the infrastructure.

These forms of legislation are an important means of protecting the community's interests through Building Regulations control over structural stability or energy consumption, or by planning control over incompatible uses or overload of the infrastructure.

The findings of *Buildings: a new life* were that legislation had other, perhaps unexpected influences on building life. For example, security of tenure provisions in one outmoded office building that had a residential element was, almost certainly, a key factor in rendering redevelopment uneconomic and causing the owners to look more creatively at opportunities for re-use. The resulting conversion to a hotel has proved successful economically and met a demand within the locality.

The issue of legislation is wide but leads to some key questions when considering a building's future life.

The Travel Inn, Euston Road, London
This building was originally designed and constructed as offices but quickly became functionally and economically obsolete; the building then became a candidate for re-development, in common with many others around it. In this case, the presence of a tenancy of the upper parts held by the local authority for social housing was a significant factor in rendering development unviable. It prompted the exploration of other uses for the building which led to conversion to a hotel.

Summary

The consideration of social sustainability will be of increasing importance in the shaping of buildings for the future. Not only does the drive towards greater social sustainability give rise to legislation that has a direct impact on the way buildings can be used but it also affects the attitudes of building owners and occupiers as they seek to improve their sustainability credentials. Already social accounting and reporting are important and growing considerations for corporate organisations and their impact on property decisions will inevitably be even greater.

In this chapter we looked at the issues from a UK perspective, rather than an international one or one embracing other cultural perspectives but many of the key issues are sufficiently generic to be transportable to any other urban environment. The current key questions are:

- Does the building allow for social and cultural adaptability?
- Of what significance is the building in cultural and social terms?
- What emotional response does the building evoke – is it 'loveable'?
- To what extent is it affected by construction legislation?
- To what extent does occupation legislation affect its future capabilities?
- Does it add to the local amenities of an area and is it appropriately served by amenities?
- Does it provide for its internal stakeholders an environment that is appropriate in social and quality terms?

Social sustainability appears to often have conflicting interests with the other two headings, the wish to retain evidence of our culture may impede the development of new buildings or public transport systems and yet in the longer term the objectives of all forms of sustainability are to preserve our society and its environment. Social objectives are hard to measure thus even harder to balance against the specific quantifiable targets which are developed for economic and environmental objectives.

Endnotes

1. The first three principles relate to *substituting* renewable materials for non-renewables; *minimising* the use of harmful or non-degradable following the principle of eco-efficiency.
2. www.bbc.co.uk/1/hi/uk/1511841.stm.

Chapter 6

The Building Sustainability Assessment Tool

Principal Messages:

- *Whether a building is really sustainable is something that can only be determined retrospectively, as the needs and requirements of future generations cannot be known. That is not a reason however to pursue a course of inaction and many decisions about buildings can be taken to provide some level of 'future proofing'.*

- *For appropriate decisions regarding the future of a building a triple bottom line (TBL) approach is advocated. The findings of the Buildings: a new life project point to the importance of social and economic factors in determining whether or not a building is likely to survive over time. It also found that the environmental agenda has not, to date, been a key to decision-making although this may change in the future as legislation which reflects changing social attitudes to the environment, begin to take effect.*

- *The concept of six 'Ls' of sustainability is fundamental to the development of understanding building sustainability. These relate to loose fit, low energy, location, longevity, likeability and loveability*

- *An understanding of sustainability is a product of the social and economic environment. Over time the issues that are perceived to be the critical ones facing a society, change and so do the solutions. With ever-changing attitudes and technology the agenda for building sustainability cannot be regarded as definitive. Flexibility and overall quality are therefore probably the most important factors to assist in the quest for sustainable buildings.*

- *A Building Sustainability Assessment Tool (BSAT) has been developed to assist stakeholders with the difficulties involved in making appropriate 'futureproof' decisions.*

- *The purpose of the BSAT toolkit is to provide a relatively straightforward framework within which stakeholders can enter a dialogue in order to reconcile the many different influences on a building and its sustainability.*

- *All properties are heterogeneous. Therefore while some of the influences on building sustainability will be clearly defined others may be based on points of perception and will they will vary from property to property. The BSAT has been designed to allow stakeholders to incorporate building specific issues as appropriate.*

- *It is apparent from the earlier chapters in this study that, despite the simplification which is often applied to the question of sustainability, many of the issues are capable of different interpretations and sometimes the different bases for consideration may be in opposition to each other. The toolkit does not seek to provide a definitive answer but to help identify the areas of conflict.*

- *Use of the toolkit is explored and the various forms of input illustrated by working through hypothetical examples.*

Drawing conclusions

In Chapters 1–5 of the this book the meaning of sustainability was investigated as it is understood today and as it relates to the built environment and, more particularly, to the context of an individual building.

Of particular concern has been the investigation of issues that do, or arguably should, inform the discussion between various stakeholders when determining the future of an existing building. Consequently, throughout the preceding chapters reference has been made to the research project carried out by the authors entitled *Buildings: a new life*. This project set out to inform the debate in respect of the factors that determine whether or not a building should be retained if triple bottom line as opposed to single bottom line principles are adopted.

In developing the research the standpoint was taken that a wide range of issues affected decisions relating to the future life of a building and that these could be broadly categorised into economic, environmental and social factors – the triple bottom line (TBL). Further, from an early stage it was recognised that buildings had two sets of stakeholders: those internal to the building, such as owners and occupiers who all have a financial involvement, direct or indirect and external stakeholders, such as the community and casual users (such as shoppers and restaurant goers). The structure of this book reflects these decisions, in that chapters have been devoted to more detailed consideration of each of the triple bottom line elements while in Chapter 2 the nature of stakeholders was discussed.

Synthesis of the issues

Longevity: more than an environmental matter

The research provided a perspective from which to approach the question: how should decisions about the future life of an existing building be taken if TBL principles are to be incorporated? From the viewpoint of energy conservation, the key role of embodied energy should point to retention wherever possible, as the energy when used is thereby amortised over as long a period as possible. This alone ensures that longevity has a key part to play

in the quest for sustainable building and is a key issue in the criticisms of HERS (Home Energy Rating Scheme) and SAP (Standard Assessment Procedure) ratings which by ignoring this factor can lead to support for LESS efficient forms of construction.

The analysis indicated clearly that the economic and social aspects of a building outweigh any environmental or energy considerations in determining its life. This analysis can be challenged as the energy factors are likely to take on far greater economic relevance with the introduction of both incentives and fiscal measures. Within the UK, however this is not currently the case. Maximum revenue saving from 'green buildings' may represent typically only a 2–3% saving on building running costs (Walker *et al.*, 2001) which is hardly enough to determine what a building owner decides should be the future of a building.

The issue of longevity goes to the heart of sustainability. To preserve buildings does not necessarily provide the right solution: cities and towns change and buildings need to adapt or be renewed. As Melet (1999:13) argues:

A living city does not consist solely of long-lasting buildings. Needs change and the city must change along with them. Besides buildings which will stand the test of time, we must develop buildings that are easy to dismantle. They must be capable of vanishing without trace to make place for new functions. It is this openness to change which makes a city sustainable.

The role of flexibility and a time dimension

The findings from the *Buildings: a new life* project demonstrate that flexibility and adaptability are critical to survival and this has been a connecting thread through all the work. The difficulty is that it is impossible to predict what configuration changes may be required of buildings as a result of both business practices and life style modes in the future. Only 20 years ago the needs of buildings were that they could accommodate the trunking and cabling required for the then new technologies which resulted in many post-war buildings being constructed with low floor to ceiling heights, ironically for energy conservation reasons, failing economically due to a lack of structural adaptability, whereas some older buildings survived. Therefore any quest to design a 'once and for all' solution in structural terms will not succeed. What is of greater importance is that the structural form can accommodate and adapt and it is only in this way that the potential economic future of the building, within its original use or any other, can be assured. Therefore the concept of 'loose fit' is instrumental to assisting building to retain usefulness.

This raises another issue: buildings can be viewed as isolated assets, individual structures built for a purpose and a resource for activity, economic or social. While they undoubtedly fulfil this role, (1) it is only part of the issue. Research has confirmed that building survival is connected to its setting and economic context which presents a difficulty, as the context will change over time.

One of the case study buildings was a converted warehouse in London Docklands. This vast tranche of land had been at the hub of the UK's import trade until the 1970s and the Port of London and its associated docks and warehousing provision had been, for over a century, the centre of manufacturing and a busy, if not always prosperous, area (O'Neill, 1999). With the closure of the docks and the move of associated industries down-river in the space of little more than a decade the system closed down leading to some 8.5 square miles of dereliction (Hall, 1996). The original use for all of the buildings was lost, but while some were listed, others were not. In respect of the case study property an application for demolition was made and rejected but ironically, it was probably only the lack of any value that led to no stronger push to demolish. The building then lay empty for some two decades, eventually being brought back into use for residential and leisure uses as the context changed – the result of publicly led development subsequently supported by private sector monies. In this case, the new life of the building, initially 'saved' from demolition by statutory intervention arose from value shift in the immediate vicinity. The new use is economically viable but it derives this from the social setting, not from its intrinsic form.

A sustainable location

The issue of location was highlighted as important in both the survey and the matrix but it is perhaps simplistic to say that location is the root of sustainability of buildings since like the economic context, location is not a static issue. It is one of the chief determinants of economic value but as with Docklands the desirability of a location is a function of accessibility, local economic activity and the less definable issues of ambience and aesthetic appeal. There remains an issue in sustainability terms as to which location is best able to support longevity and which is preferred on environmental grounds. On environmental grounds a sustainable building location must be one that minimises the need for transport, especially private transport, with its adverse impact in terms of energy consumption, pollution and congestion. As a corollary, new buildings should inherently be more sustainable if they do not offer the possibility of car parking and are located close to public transport nodes. To the financial (internal) stakeholders however the need for car parking remains an important feature without which economic value will not be maximised thus threatening sustainability.

The dilemma of location is played out on a larger scale in relation to city size. The advocates of sustainable cities often advocate the compact form (Elkin *et al.*, 1991) although Hall (1996) casts some doubt on the validity of this proposition. The paradox is that as the demand grows for compact human scale settlements, in which the familiar (and by implication traditional) structural forms prevail, the reality has been an explosion of mega-cities and the continuing concentration of urban activity. Although it is outside the scope of this book to debate the reasons for this, the views of Beauregard and Haila (2000) are relevant. They argue that real estate assets have become both dissociated from their locality (in that ownership is concentrated in global investors) and deeply commodified so that value lies increasingly in a property's performance as a financial asset separately from its social and utility function.

These trends, which have been seen within the UK over many years (Massey and Catalano, 1978; Plender, 1982) have facilitated the financial structures which lead to a concentration of large-scale developments within or at the edges of mega-centre cities and which demand ever increasing building floor plates. Here, the demand for buildings of size sufficient to accommodate global enterprises leads to an increase in land values such that older stock, however adaptable in specification and form, may be ousted by the increased financial returns consequent on economies of scale. As Henneberry (1996) argues, investment values are determined,

by investors based mainly in London seeking investments... appear to be largely insensitive to spatio-temporal variation in the behaviour of property users as revealed by local rents.

The issue of building form is almost irrelevant.

In the face of these trends, the survivability of buildings may be threatened by the strong economic performance of a locality just as easily as loss of economic wealth in an area can threaten value and so building life. Research has not provided an answer to this dilemma but the analysis fits with a discernible trend in relation to the nature of wealth-creation buildings, as compared with wealth-consuming buildings. The former is at the hub of economic activity and they may demand new, highly specific buildings, fit for specialised purpose. Global businesses have tended to require ever larger (increasingly sized) buildings, compatible with their worldwide image (Insignia Richard Ellis, 2002).

Sustainable buildings: fit for purpose and liked by community

It is within major owner-occupied wealth-creation sectors that the most energy efficient buildings have been specified but much wealth consuming activity can be accommodated in the re-used building; indeed the exploitation of the old can add to the 'offer' in terms of leisure and retail and living activity. Not only is longevity of buildings achieved but a re-definition of the role and character of the town or city leads to a feeling of permanence and security (Sustainable Development Commission, 2001). The key to survival can be expressed in terms of the ways in which a building can stimulate an emotional response from the external stakeholders. This can be described as the 'lovability' factor. Although the survey respondents did not rate this factor as important, the case studies provided significant evidence that it is.

The temporal context of sustainability

One of the major difficulties in achieving sustainable buildings is that sustainability is about 'future proofing' and so is almost by definition an unachievable goal. In this chapter a tool is described to help in the debate. It must be recognised however that no tool will provide easy solutions to the decision as to which buildings to demolish and which to retain. This is the real issue: as Bell and Morse (1999) argue in the final analysis sustainability is incapable of measurement. The term is at best subjective. How something is viewed today will inevitably be a product of today's values.

In assessing the importance of aids to sustainability this aspect of the cultural, economic and technological context is important. These can change slowly or by external shocks. For example, the Victorians were jolted by the cholera outbreaks of the 1830s and 1840s into considering the sustainability of their towns. Their main pre-occupation became one of health improvement and this was reflected in the establishment in 1844 of the Health of Towns Association. Open sewers, lack of potable water, back-to-back housing with poor ventilation, and other similar problems, all produced a focus on air, light and hygiene as the most important issues in creating a sustainable city.

Later, recognition of the value of sunlight, open spaces and well ventilated buildings in terms of productivity was first reflected in planning by the Garden City Movement and then in the plans for new towns after the second World War. The swing however was too great and they created enclaves which were almost entirely reliant on private transport to sustain their economic and social life: Milton Keynes is a typical example of a town with extreme dependence on the motor car, something that in today's climate of concerns about depletion of natural resources and adverse ecological effects, renders inappropriate the solution enacted just a few decades ago.

Today, external shocks such as a run of severe weather conditions, have highlighted the need for environmental regulation, while social change dictates an agenda built on recognition of the community. These can be seen in both government policy and in statute. It is not just the agenda that is subject to change however the technological solutions available today were not open to previous generations. The spread of infectious diseases that led to better infrastructure has, within the UK at least, been largely replaced by advances in medical science as the prime mechanism of control.

Today's concern with environment and energy

focus on the depletion and emissions issues but, as recognised by Lovins *et al.*, (1999) advances in technology mean that the use of fossil fuels may decline or cease as renewable sources become more advanced and economic. If in the next century, the technology could exist for 100% carbon-emission free energy, then the whole agenda on which the current quest for 'green' buildings is founded would vanish. Given that the design life of buildings is normally perceived to be in excess of 50 years, a concentration on one issue over all others is probably misplaced.

So, for true sustainability, buildings must be capable not only of displaying the characteristics set out above, but must also be able to display them over time. They are not capable of definition in terms of their low energy consumption or indeed a particular characteristic that has captured either the public or government's attention. There is

much truth in the argument expounded by Melet (1999:13) that

Perhaps pleasing, multifaceted buildings and neighbourhoods that challenge and stimulate us are more important than a low EPC.(2) Buildings have to hold the attention of the short attention-span zapping generation. They must resist the throwaway society so that they can continue functioning long into the future. By combining these attributes with architectural solutions to limit energy consumption and indeed to generate energy, it is these that will be the genuinely sustainable buildings.

In conclusion, the lesson to be learnt from the past is that sustainability issues change all the time and focusing on one issue can lead to other problems in the future. With changing attitudes and technology the agenda for building sustainability cannot be regarded as definitive, flexibility and high quality are therefore probably the most important factors to assist in the quest for sustainable

Specialised Building Types: former cinema, Ashford, Middlesex
This cinema, which formed one of the case studies, has proved to be unsustainable for its original use. The very specific nature of the form of this building restricted the alternative uses to which it could be put and ultimately led to its demolition. Modern cinemas with their stadium seating can be even more restrictive and measures to ensure that they can be converted to open space at a later stage are generally not economically sustainable. For some of these types of use the ability to take a building to pieces and reuse either components or their constituent materials may be the most sustainable option.

buildings and to overcome the uncertainty inherent in the temporal aspect of sustainability.

The application of the Buildings Sustainability Assessment Tool

There are a number of tests such as the DETR sponsored *Office Scorer* produced by the BRE (www.officescorer.info; Anderson and Mills, 2002), but they mainly provide an isolated snapshot of a specific aspect of a building and while important in their own right, have no methodology for relating their results to the wider context in which the building sits. Similarly there are assessment tools to assist when a new building project is to be carried out (see for example see www.sustainability-checklist.co.uk).

Most tests also fail to recognise the different, and often conflicting, concerns of different stakeholder groups but it has been identified above that the quest for sustainable solutions requires the needs of external stakeholders be included . The *Buildings: a new life* study concluded that in creating a better awareness of the issues and a total appreciation of the true sustainability of a building or an area, a framework is required within which the various studies can be related.

Such a process is not of interest to students and academics only; for the commercial developer there is an increasing demand for a sustainability plan as part of the selection process for town centre developments or for achieving a planning consent. For practitioners obligations are being imposed to create sustainable buildings, for the community there is a direct interest in being able to assess the impact of a proposal, and for the user it can be of assistance in determining the cost of occupying a particular space, or indeed as a contribution to their business profile.

The Building Sustainability Assessment Tool devised in the light of this research recognises that the user must be able to work with different levels of data within an assessment and it provides a framework within which the various isolated specialist results can be related to the overall sustainability. It also seeks to encompass different criteria for different buildings, and it provides a means of weighting the results to reflect the relative importance of different issues.

It is also recognised that the test must be suitable for different situations, from that of an individual wishing to make an assessment of a specific building to a group exercise with representatives of several different stakeholders taking part in the evaluation.

No test is sufficient in itself to determine the fate of a building but it does give guidelines and highlight the issues to be resolved, thereby removing many time wasting discussions. Indeed by raising awareness of the issues it may go a long way towards resolving them.

The assessment is based on the key diagram which informed the study from the outset. The two axes represent the internal and external stakeholders' interests. Where there is unanimity in evaluation the format produces a simple answer of either retention more or less intact or at the other end outright demolition but it is recognised that this will be a rare event and the test is designed to highlight the relevant points of dissension.

The test procedure, set out below, covers a wide range of situations of which the following are examples:

- Initial appraisal of a building by the owner, developer, consultant or local authority in preparing a design or development brief.
- Support in a planning application. Here the test could be used either by the applicant or the local authority, jointly or in isolation.
- Use by local conservation/residents groups to assist in determining whether to support or resist a planning application or a new UDP (Unitary Development Plan).
- As an appraisal in considering work to a listed building to achieve the difficult balance between alteration and retention of original fabric.
- In support of public grant aid for historic buildings where the test provides an indication that support, either in the form of financial aid or a relaxation of other conditions, is necessary to ensure the buildings' survival.

The Building Sustainability Assessment Tool

The Building Sustainability Assessment Tool is based on the concept that a building's future will be determined by a number of forces which may be broadly described under the headings of internal or external stakeholder influences. The latter incorporates interests such as the local or wider community and the cultural values or specific legislation involved, while the internal forces will be governed by the building owner, the tenants and the users (see Chapter 2).

A series of questions are answered from the viewpoints of the internal and the external stakeholders. These can be completed either as initial reactions or, where appropriate, by use of detailed assessment. There are for example a number of programmes for measuring energy consumption which can be used as a basis for scoring in the matrix. As far as general appeal is concerned, a survey could be carried out which would identify the degree of success or otherwise of a building both among its occupants and in the community. As a study develops, answers can be replaced by more specific and measured responses, gradually refining the assessment process and providing a mechanism for feedback. Scoring is in a range from 1 to 5, the higher score indicating greater success in satisfying the particular issue under consideration.

As set out above, a range of issues has been identified through the survey carried out for the *Buildings: a new life* research project. For the purposes of the Building Sustainability Assessment Tool, these have been grouped under the three headings of the triple bottom line and are amplified in the earlier chapters at the end of which are a series of seven key questions designed to embrace the range of factors taken into account. For ease of reference these key questions are reproduced at the end of this chapter. It is however recognised that different issues may arise in a particular project and it is anticipated that the range of questions would be adjusted to suit specific needs.

Similar flexibility is possible with the selection of respondents. The survey can be carried out by an individual wishing to establish in broad principle the issues to be considered for a planning application, or by groups representing different stakeholders.

The relationship is shown in Figure 6.1 from which can four sectors can be identified. At the extremes A and C there is common ground between both internal and external forces: in C the building is of little or no value and would be better redeveloped, whereas in A the building is of

Figure 6.1: Internal and external sustainability: the conceptual relationship grid

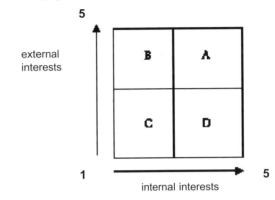

1 indicates failure and 5 success in satisfying the criteria

considerable value to the community as well as to the user/owner and should remain intact as far as possible.

Most buildings probably lie somewhere within B or D and so are of greater interest. In these areas the general indication is that the building should be retained, perhaps allowing for radical alteration or possibly with the aim of attracting publicly funded support.

Sector B contains buildings which may be of considerable interest to the community for their cultural value, in providing employment or for other reasons, but whose viability is jeopardised by significant environmental problems. In these cases the building fabric will generally be retained but changes of use may be appropriate, or public or charitable funding sought to help in modernisation or conservation of the fabric.

Sector D contains buildings which are considered by the community to be undesirable: for example they may be aesthetically unappealing, environmentally damaging, or an obstruction to other plans, but which provide useful accommodation for their users. Here radical alteration to improve the appearance or to mitigate any nuisance may be sought to enable the building to become economically viable in their own right.

In practice the areas of certainty are smaller and there is a need for a more gradual transition between the four quadrants as shown in Figure 6.2 where the bottom left hand segment represents a concenus for demolition and the top right-hand a consensus for conservation or retention. The band in between represents retention with varying

Figure 6.2: The relationship grid

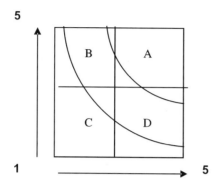

degrees of intervention and/or community financial support.

The issues can be assessed using the grid to give a visual analysis of the issues where points falling within the different sectors provide an indication for the future of the building and the areas of difference. This does not however allow different weightings to be attributed to specific topics and a mathematical matrix has been developed to achieve a more sensitive analysis while retaining the simplicity of the original concept.

Each issue in the matrix is scored from one to five where five indicates that the building satisfies the criterion and one that it fails to do so and each is scored from the perspective of both the internal and external stakeholders. In some cases a particular question or group of issues may be considered to have a disproportionate importance for a particular building and there is provision for a weighting of 1 [standard] up to 3 [major significance] to be used in column 5 (see p96 onwards).

The scoring matrix provides a simple numerical analysis to determine in which sector the building lies and to allow alternative scenarios to be tested. The matrix is in the form of a simple spreadsheet (see inserted disc in back pocket). The score is calculated automatically on entry of the data. Thus the matrix provides an overall score which is also shown by the triple bottom line categories, and will also highlight issues where there is a significant variation between internal and external views.

The following questions are recommended as providing a core of issues to be considered and have been prepared using the results of surveys into key issues. There may well be alternative or

additional questions to be raised for a specific building but it is recommended that the balance between economic, social and environmental issues is maintained. In preparing additional questions the scope of the question should be identified clearly to ensure that respondents understand the issues fully and it is also important that the range of points to be considered by internal and external stakeholders be listed.

Economic

E1   Does the building work efficiently?

Scope: This question seeks to identify whether the building is wasteful through inefficient use of space, of resources or by creating waste in its occupier's organisation. In other words it will establish whether it is fit for purpose.

Internal stakeholders: It is important for the building owner and the occupiers that as large a proportion as possible of the building area should contribute to the activities which take place. At the most fundamental level this is a measure of net useable to gross built space but for some building uses (shopping centres or niche hotels) generous circulation space may be a critical part of an enjoyable experience and thus an intrinsic part of the long term attractiveness and sustainability of the building. Depending on the nature of the building it may be necessary to consider both aspects.

External stakeholders: External stakeholders share an interest in the efficiency of the building in creating employment or providing a service to the community. At the same time the building may provide spaces or activities which contribute to the efficient or beneficial working of the community such as the opportunity to window shop at night or the provision of shop mobility facilities in a shopping centre.

E2   Does the building show an economic rate of return?

Scope: This will show whether the building provides a rate of return on the capital invested comparable with other sources of income. If the building is not a satisfactory investment in terms of income, prospective capital growth, stability and other factors then finance will not be available for its support and it will ultimately fall into decay. This will apply to buildings both in the public and private sectors, although the mechanism for determining the rate of return may differ between stakeholders.

Internal stakeholders: For the building owner the return may be a simple institutional valuation or for an owner-occupier with an historic ownership an assessment of other opportunities which may be available. For the occupier the return is an assessment of whether the total cost of occupation rent/rates/ service charge, fitting out costs etc. is viable in their business plan, combined with the degree to which space can be sublet and therefore overheads varied to meet changing circumstances. In the public sector concerns about the evaluation of the return may involve other methods such as social cost-benefit analysis.

External stakeholders: The capital employed by the external stakeholders may be grant aid, and/or infrastructure costs and the return may be measured by job creation, recovery of polluted land, rates income, increased tourism or the ability to attract inward investment.

E3 Is it an efficient use of the land?

Scope: While the built area of the UK may be only a small proportion of the total land area, there is a growing realisation that wasteful use has enormous side effects in additional travel time which affects the quality of life and the national energy consumption. Issues such as the use of previously developed land and the protection of the green belt are also aspects of inefficient use of land. Efficient management is a key concern within Agenda 21.

Internal stakeholders: For the building owner the efficient use of the land has the double aspect of quantitative maximisation of the built area against land purchased, combined with achieving a suitable quality of space to make the building competitive.

External stakeholders: Underdeveloped land will as a general rule increase travel but for the external stakeholders the efficient use of the land should include consideration of disruption and disturbance to others including interruption of sunlight, winds/ downdrafts etc.

E4 The effect of the form of property tenure

Scope: Property tenure has several aspects. It covers site/building specific covenants, easements and/or other binding constraints which may be reflected in the rent paid, the building costs and the property value. Important among these may be leasing arrangements. It is not intended that this should cover planning, heritage or employment legislation which are included under social issues.

Internal stakeholders: Restrictions might include agreements not to infringe light or views, to have a nil settlement provision if building over underground services or for the occupier may be reflected in the lease provisions which restrict the hours of use, type of activity, level of rent achievable, security of tenure etc.

External stakeholders: Restrictions might be environmental such as lack of access, and decline in the amenity of an area consequent on land owner restrictions and resulting neglect

E5 The quality of the transport access

Scope: Suitable access to a building is essential whether it be for workers or for delivery of goods. Decisions about occupation and ownership and thus its long term sustainability will be influenced by the quality of transport available to the site by public or private means. Increasingly quality of transport access implies both public and private transport links.

Internal stakeholders: Reliable public transport and periods when it is available will be important, the quality depending on the nature of the activity. For example, leisure users will be more concerned about evening and late night transport while in industrial locations there may be more concern about the scope for large vehicles and any width or weight restrictions. The use of private transport will be less significant in town centre locations for big conurbations but more significant in smaller towns which draw employment from country areas, and in suburban locations serving a wider range than the immediate walking distance.

External stakeholders: The quality of transport access determines the degree of access the public have to the building. For example, a planning department in the centre of the town but remote from cross-borough transport does not serve the community well. To be sustainable, buildings that serve the public should be located to be accessible to all potential users, including those who have access only to public transport and those with mobility difficulties or other disabilities.

E6 Building fabric maintenance/durability

Scope: The fabric, including service installations, is essential to the survival of the building and its sustainability. Traditional materials and services can generally be repaired or maintained on a piecemeal basis but more modern equipment and prefabricated cladding systems rely on the availability of components. Traditional repairs can generally be carried out by local tradesmen thus providing employment and reducing travelling costs while prefabricated elements, even when available, are often sourced on an international basis.

Internal stakeholders: For the building owner the durability of the fabric and the ability to repair it represents a maintenance cost which can affect the viability of the investment. For example, glass roofs without proper access can be expensive to clean but if left dirty will in the long term affect the performance of the glass and impair the appearance of the building.

External stakeholders: For the community the appearance of the building can add or detract from the quality of the environment. Building maintenance can be a useful source of local

employment but if international prefabricated systems are used this opportunity may be denied.

E7 Building adaptability

Scope: The ability of a building to adapt to changing circumstances is essential to its survival and sustainability. Because of its importance and the variety of ways in which a building can adapt this is an issue under each aspect of the triple bottom line. Under the economic heading, adaptability reflects the flexibility for modification at a viable cost.

Internal stakeholders: Inflexible structures and forms of construction as well as deleterious materials all have a cost implication in adapting the building to meet changing needs. Size and depth of building are two characteristics of form that may not be able to be changed depending on site and planning constraints and on the basic building design.

External stakeholders: New infrastructure may be needed to meet changing needs for such things as deliveries or the production of waste.

Social

S1 Adaptability

Scope: Part of a building's adaptability reflects changing social demands from the disappearance of servants in domestic accommodation to changing structures in the office moving from cellular defensible space to hot desking.

Internal stakeholders: The social structures within organisations change over time and the ability of the building to adapt to these pressures can play an important role in the organisation's evolution. If the space is not adaptable either the occupier will have to move on and be replaced by another – possibly with a different use – or the building is no longer sustainable.

External stakeholders: The building may need to be adaptable to changing social patterns – primary industries have largely made way to service and leisure users. Both working and shopping habits have also changed leading to different uses of buildings.

S2 Cultural importance

Scope: Society recognises the importance of some buildings through the listing system and the use of Conservation Areas. This is as part of the cultural heritage. Buildings may have value in social terms, not for their functional importance but for the vital role they may have to play in the local community or in creating tourist attractions and with consequent economic implications. In addition to the national interest there may be local lists indicating that while the building form may not be sufficiently unique to warrant national protection it is seen to be of significance for the immediate community.

Internal stakeholders: Listing affects the use of the building even if only in the need to obtain consent for many forms of alteration. This has a cost and time penalty and so generally listing for commercial buildings will be seen as a restriction which inhibits its commercial value. Some uses however may derive positive benefit from the building being listed, including residential and leisure activities. For instance, the latter can make use of the atmosphere provided by an historic building or quarter of the town. Some building users have found an indirect benefit whereby in having to look more carefully at what is permitted they have improved their use of space. For the building owner the major downside is that listing is likely to prevent or delay any redevelopment proposals for the site.

External stakeholders: For the community the protection of the historic environment has positive benefits in retaining the qualities of the town and also potentially in reducing disturbance from construction traffic, but it is also important to ensure that there is an adequate supply of suitable accommodation for the commercial vitality of the area. An over protected environment may blight areas and have a bad affect on the sustainability of individual buildings. If the building is important to the community then community funding may be needed to maintain it but it should be born in mind that a building retained but unused does not improve the vitality of the neighbourhood.

S3 Appeal (loveability and likeability)

Scope: A building which genuinely appeals to its users or to the local community is more likely to be maintained and to be sustainable. Listing, favourable references in the press or technical publications may provide an indication of social significance and more formal investigations could include reference to local conservation groups. For internal stakeholders there are unlikely to be similar measures although staff absentee records or complaints may provide a rough guide. For both groups a simple survey can be carried out to give a more precise measure.

Internal stakeholders: Various studies have shown that a working environment which is popular improves productivity and reduces the number of absentees. Buildings which are loved are more likely to be cared for by both the owners and the occupiers.

External stakeholders: Buildings which are loved will generally obtain support from local pressure groups if there are proposals to demolish or sometimes to even modify them. Buildings of little national interest can often have strong local support but the community has an interest in retaining a vital economy and creating the heritage for the future and alteration and even demolition may be the best means of achieving these aims.

S4 Construction Legislation – planning and building regulations

Scope: This discussion of legislation is intended to cover that which deals with social issues such as planning, construction and building conservation.

Internal stakeholders: In addition to the constraints on the use, alteration or development of a particular building under the planning legislation the capacity of a building to respond to legislation such that concerning access for the disabled has an important impact on the ability of the occupier to use the space.

External stakeholders: These forms of legislation are an important means of protecting the community's interests through Building Regulations control over structural stability or energy consumption and by planning control over incompatible uses or overload of the infrastructure.

S5 Occupation legislation

Scope: This legislative issue is intended to cover general legislation which deals with social issues affecting the use of the property including licensing, access for the disabled and employment.

Internal stakeholders: In addition to the constraints on the use, alteration or development of a particular building under the planning legislation, the ability of a building to respond to legislation such as the access for the disabled has an important impact on the ability of the occupier to use the space. Increasingly, the need to meet CSR policy issues will affect an occupier (and an investor's) attitude towards a building.

External stakeholders: These forms of legislation are an important means of protecting the community's interests as users or potential employees in a building to ensure that working conditions, safety of the buildings users or a fair and equal basis of employment is maintained.

S6 Locality

Scope: The commercial development community has held to the mantra of location, location, location as being fundamental to a successful development. Community uses have similar pressures and a building which is badly located will suffer by being un-used, abused or just missed. Some forms of use will be more susceptible than others, discretionary uses such as leisure and most retailing have to be in the right location or, as at Bluewater or the Eden project; to create their location. Other uses such as housing are not fundamentally so sensitive to location but will be equally affected in terms of their value.

Internal stakeholders: The perceived quality of the area for the particular activity and the range of local amenities will be of interest to the occupiers and thus to the building owners.

External stakeholders: For the community the

question is a matter of the degree to which the building and its users contribute to the quality of the local environment.

S7 Working environment quality

Scope: The quality to be considered is not lighting, cooling etc which are covered under environmental concerns: here we consider the more abstract qualities of design, layout and social integration.

Internal stakeholders: The general quality of the environment has been recognised in some of the issues above and here the intention is to establish how the current environment meets needs and expectations.

External stakeholders: The external stakeholders have less interest in the internal environment apart from the degree to which it provides suitable and pleasant employment opportunities.

Environmental

En1 Standards

Scope: The quality of the environment both internally and externally to the building can have a significant distinct effect on the occupier experience from the viewpoint of both productivity and the satisfaction of the users, whether they be internal stakeholders, such as employers or external stakeholders such as visitors to a shopping centre or leisure destination. In addition there are statutory standards which must be maintained and which, according to the building's form and construction, may or may not be achieved. Increasingly these are likely to place pressures on buildings that are inflexible or which lack good amenities such as natural light.

Internal stakeholders: There are legal standards, which have to be met for most employment activities, and the building must meet these criteria in order to be sustainable. The internal stakeholder is also affected in terms of satisfaction and usability.

External stakeholders: Environmental standards have an impact on the community through the emissions, that it makes and through the quality of finishes, such as glare from curtain walling.

En2 Energy consumption

Scope: Energy. The importance of energy consumption to the global community cannot be doubted but running costs are often only a small part of the occupier's budget. The issue of energy consumption is linked both to the depletion of natural resources and to that of carbon emissions. The issue of energy consumption relates primarily to the use of the building through direct means such as heating and cooling, replacement of components, maintenance and the energy related to travel to the building. Over time the implementation of government strategy, both national and supranational is towards enforcement policies and fiscal measures to reduce carbon emissions both by reducing energy consumption and shifting it to renewable sources. Therefore over time non-energy efficient buildings are likely to become increasingly unsustainable.

Internal stakeholders: To the internal stakeholder the energy consumption issue is one of costs of occupation. At present these costs are not usually significant in the overall business plan but it may be anticipated that they could become so. For the building owner, increasingly severe regulations regarding heat loss and air seepage are beginning to have an effect and as these apply to alterations that effect may increase. Currently energy consumption related to accessing the building is not factored in to decision-making.

External stakeholders: The issue for the external community is largely one of global warming, pollution from energy consumption and using up natural resources at a faster rate than they can be renewed.

En3 Embodied energy

Scope: This heading relates to the energy that is expended through the construction process and consequently trapped in the building. Embodied energy is 'lost' when a building is demolished and a new building takes its place. The issues therefore relates to building life cycles. Promotion of a longer life will provide a longer period over which the energy use can be amortised. This is unlikely to be of significance to the occupier and only slightly to the owner unless some form of energy tax is placed on new construction. For the community however it is significant, not only in the global warming energy impact from the production of new materials but also in the energy consumed in demolition and in transport of waste from the site and in bringing new products to it.

Internal stakeholders: For the occupier tenant embodied energy has little significance. For the owner it could become an issue with redevelopment. It is also an influence in terms of refurbishment cycles.

External stakeholders: The issue of embodied energy is a significant one for the community at large. In many cases it would be better to permit more radical alterations to existing buildings so that they can satisfy particular demands in the locality rather than seeking to preserve them unchanged and so force the requirement for new accommodation to be provided elsewhere. Conversely, the approach of little and often could ensure that a building is kept in use for a maximum period of time, thereby gaining efficiency in embodied energy terms.

En4 Materials and Pollutants

Scope: The nature of the materials in a building will contribute to the environmental impact the building has on its surroundings and in general sustainability terms. While asbestos is probably the best known hazardous material there are a number of others, many of which were not known to present a risk when first used. Service systems may present risks either through disposal of air conditioning refrigerants or in lack of proper maintenance causing Legionnaires Disease or other hazards. Manufacturing processes in particular can have unacceptable by-products or emissions. To replace these will in some instances require the demolition of a substantial part of the building or it may limit the use of areas of the building, rendering it unsustainable to both user and community. Additionally some materials are capable of re-use whereas others create environmental issues in connection with waste.

Internal stakeholders: The building must provide a safe working environment. The definition of precisely what constitutes a hazard changes frequently and the degree of risk assessment in a building will have an impact on its long term use and sustainability. To the owner the issue of waste management both in use and during the refurbishment or redevelopment process is gaining importance.

External stakeholders: The community has an interest in limiting risks not only as a social obligation but also because treatment is a cost to society. Additionally, the matter of material re-use has implications in terms of resource depletion.

En5 Environmental quality of the location including the effect of transport systems

Scope: A location where there is pollution, an aggressive environment, adverse winds or other similar issues is likely to be demanding on the building fabric and to increase maintenance costs. It may shorten the life of building components and thus bring forward the point at which substantial renewal or development becomes an issue. The various forms of transport which are based on the use of fossil fuels are major contributors to pollution and global warming and while they do not directly affect the building itself they do contribute to its overall impact and should therefore be taken into account. The energy consumption aspect is covered in item En2 but the question of more general pollution and its impact on the quality of the environment is covered under this head.

Internal stakeholders: A poor environment which is due to traffic noise, dirt etc will have an impact on whether windows can be opened and thus the need for artificial means of ventilation. It will also affect the sense of well-being and productivity including economic success.

External stakeholders: The issues which concern the community are very similar to those which concern the occupier. Their interest lies in whether the existing building or a replacement would better mitigate adverse environmental effects.

En6 Ecological issues

Scope: Buildings have a wide-ranging impact on the local and national ecology from roosting places for bats, to creating micro-climates which may support or reject natural life forms. Buildings in town centres are less likely to be directly affected.

Internal stakeholders: For the building owner the impact of the local ecology may be mainly an adverse one where protected species, such as bats, cannot be disturbed.

External stakeholders: The community usually has a vested interest in protecting the local ecology. Over time this may lead to greater legislative measures

En7 Adaptability

Scope: The adaptability of the building to meet new technologies is a major consideration both economically and in terms of the building environmental quality. The ability to adapt to changing working practices, is important in determining whether or not a building will live. It is notable that while new technologies impose new demands since so much of the building stock is older, solutions can be found to many technology problems, given an appropriate economic case.

Internal stakeholders: For the building users it is essential that the building can meet the technical needs and environmental needs of their business. For the investing owner adapt-ability is not an issue, unless the building is so specialised that it makes the likelihood of other tenants taking the space remote. There-fore, even to investing owners, adaptability is a concern.

External stakeholders: The community needs to maintain a balanced workforce and so has an interest in ensuring that the accommod-ation in its area can support the latest technologies within working environments that are socially acceptable.

Assessing the results

A score of 6 or below indicates that the building is considered to be of low if any value by both the internal and external stakeholders. There is little reason therefore to retain the building and its redevelopment is to be welcomed. The benefit of splitting the scores into the triple bottom line groups is that it can be seen that while there are social and environmental reasons for development there may be no economic justification and that it may be necessary to consider where the project lies in the general economic cycle since although not viable now it may become so at a later date. Conversely if a building is not valued because of social or environmental issues, these are less likely to change and may provide a clear indication for redevelopment and pointers as to what form of development might be appropriate.

A score above 12 might show that the building should be retained largely intact and a proper conservation/maintenance programme put into place. Again the split into groups will help to identify whether the overriding issues are social or environmental, perhaps justifying community expenditure to deal with the unsustainable issues.

A score between 6 and 12 requires further examination. Where the total external score exceeds the internal score it will probably be necessary to seek assistance from the community in the form of financial support or by permitting change of use or other relaxations in order to achieve a viable future. If the total internal score exceeds the external then it is clear that the building can be radically altered and adapted but is unlikely to be redeveloped because of its current value to the owner/occupier.

Having identified a broad future for the building, examination of the areas where there is a significant difference between the external and internal scores will assist in identifying future actions and the areas of potential gain through mutual cooperation. The matrix has a star system to highlight the areas of greatest difference.

Applying the Building Sustainability Assessment Tool: an hypothetical example 1

To illustrate the use of the matrix, a trial building has been taken as the basis for an example, but altered in certain respects to provide anonymity.

The hypothetical building is used for higher education in a prosperous suburb of a major city. It has a tower and lower buildings. Built in the 1960s it is now in need of considerable investment to bring it up to date and to deal with major repairs to the fabric and services. The site is in a strong residential area but remote from the some of the other buildings in the faculty. Consideration needs to be given to the future of the building, to the repairs and maintenance, to extension and re-furbishment, demolition and rebuilding or alter-natively sale and/or development for other uses.

The complex has developed with a series of only partly integrated buildings which have resulted in complex and inefficient circulation and depend-ence on one ancient lift to serve the tower block. The tower is out of scale with the neighbouring area and would probably not be allowed if a similar application were made today. The site is intensively used with little landscaping or amenities although there are some attractive features along the boundary.

The matrix Figure 6.3 (Example 1) has been completed for its existing use, using a combination of factual information and estimates where this is not available: it shows that the building, having an overall score of just over 6, is not a certain candidate for demolition and redevelopment. Examination of the individual triple bottom line shows a significant variation in both the social and the environmental indicators providing a clear indicator for demolition while the economic factors indicate retention although the building is not an outstandingly successful example.

It is clear that if the building is going to be retained there will need to be significant expenditure on the fabric which may in turn affect the economic balance. One item is highlighted as representing a strong difference of opinion between the internal and external stakeholders and that is the functional adaptability of the building. This is because the internal stakeholders perceive the building according to their own use

Figure 6.3: Example 1

BUILDINGS: A NEW LIFE

Tool kit
The explanation of the question headings should be read before completing the matrix.

Scoring
1 = The building performs very badly
2 = The building performs badly
3 = The building performs neither badly nor well
4 = The building performs well
5 = The building performs outstandingly well

Weighting. If the issue is particularly significant a weighting of up to three can be applied.
Sensitivity. *** indicates a considerable difference between internal and external stakeholders

Questions	External 1–5	Internal 1–5	Ext. × Int.		(E×I)/W	Sensitivity E–I
Economic						
1 Is the building efficient	3	2	6	1	6	–
2 Is there an economic return	2	4	8	1	8	*
3 Is it efficient land use	4	3	12	1	12	–
4 Form of tenure	3	5	15	1	15	*
5 Quality of transport access	3	4	12	1	12	–
6 Maintenance of fabric	2	1	2	1	2	–
7 Functional adaptability	5	1	5	1	5	***
Average figures	3.14	2.86	8.57		8.57	–
Social						
1 Cultural adaptability	3	2	6	1	6	–
2 Cultural importance	1	1	1	1	1	–
3 Lovability	1	2	2	1	2	–
4 Construction Legislation	2	1	2	1	2	–
5 Occupation legislation	3	4	12	1	12	–
6 Local Amenities	3	1	3	1	3	*
7 Quality of work environment	3	1	3	1	3	*
Average figures	2.29	1.71	4.14		4.14	–
Environmental						
1 Environmental standards	3	2	6	1	6	–
2 Energy – consumption	3	3	9	1	9	–
3 Energy – embodied	2	5	10	1	10	**
4 Hazardous/deleterious	3	1	3	1	3	*
5 Environmental quality	3	2	6	1	6	–
6 Ecological	1	1	1	1	1	–
7 Technological adaptability	4	1	4	1	4	**
Average figures	2.71	2.14	5.57		5.57	–
Total	**2.71**	**2.24**	**6.10**		**6.10**	

Figure 6.4: Example 1 with weighting added

BUILDINGS: A NEW LIFE

Tool kit
The explanation of the question headings should be read before completing the matrix.

Scoring
1 = The building performs very badly
2 = The building performs badly
3 = The building performs neither badly nor well
4 = The building performs well
5 = The building performs outstandingly well

Weighting. If the issue is particularly significant a weighting of up to three can be applied.
Sensitivity. *** indicates a considerable difference between internal and external stakeholders

Questions	External 1–5	Internal 1–5	Ext. × Int.	(E×I)/W		Sensitivity E–I
Economic						
1 Is the building efficient	3	2	6	3	18	–
2 Is there an economic return	2	4	8	3	24	*
3 Is it efficient land use	4	3	12	1	12	–
4 Form of tenure	3	5	15	1	15	*
5 Quality of transport access	3	4	12	3	36	–
6 Maintenance of fabric	2	1	2	1	2	–
7 Functional adaptability	5	1	5	3	15	***
Average figures	3.14	2.86	8.57		8.13	
-						
Social						
1 Cultural adaptability	3	2	6	1	6	–
2 Cultural importance	1	1	1	1	1	–
3 Lovability	1	2	2	2	4	–
4 Construction legislation	2	1	2	1	2	–
5 Occupation legislation	3	4	12	1	12	–
6 Local amenities	3	1	3	3	9	*
7 Quality of work environment	3	1	3	3	9	*
Average figures	2.29	1.71	4.14		3.58	
Environmental						
1 Environmental standards	3	2	6	2	12	–
2 Energy – consumption	3	3	9	1	9	–
3 Energy – embodied	2	5	10	1	10	**
4 Hazardous/deleterious	3	1	3	1	3	*
5 Environmental quality	3	2	6	1	6	–
6 Ecological	1	1	1	1	1	–
7 Technological adaptability	4	1	4	3	12	**
Average figures	2.71	2.14	5.57		5.30	–
Total	**2.71**	**2.24**	**6.10**		**5.67**	

and needs, while the external community recognises that the building could adapt to residential use making its failure to adapt to current educational needs less significant. A similar difference arises with respect to technological adaptability although to a lesser degree. There are also two factions within the internal stakeholder community, those who use and those who own the facility, for some owner occupiers this may be of little significance but large owner occupier organisations there can be significant differences in objectives and interests between the two.

It has been recognised that some issues may be of greater significance than others and in this case the adaptability and quality of the environment are for example seen to be of considerable importance. If a weighting is added into column 5 the picture changes and the building from being a marginal candidate for retention probably with major alterations, becomes a more likely candidate for demolition and redevelopment. (See Figure 6.4.)

The overall conclusion that emerges from this analysis is that the building should be redeveloped. It is not liked by either the users or the community and has a number of environmental draw backs. The analysis does show that the economic argument by itself would not necessarily come to the same conclusion, the form of tenure is such that it does not inhibit the use of the building and possibly rather than demolition a refurbishment could take place with a change of use. When the environmental issues are examined, the embodied energy in the building does weigh in favour of retention but other factors such as deleterious materials effect it adversely. Accordingly it is a building very much in the balance.

If the assumption is that the building is to be demolished then the difference between internal and external perceptions for E7 are not important but the different views on the site use may indicate that there will be conflict in a future alternative use with the internal users considering that it is not efficient while the external stakeholders feel that it is.

Applying the Building Sustainability Assessment Tool: example 2

For the sake of comparison another higher education building is used. This is located a few miles away from the first in a suburb with a similar economic context; here the building is older and includes sections which are listed and it also needs substantial investment in the repair and maintenance of the fabric and the existing user wishes to move in order to consolidate activities at another site. The building again is in a residential area but here it is generally felt to contribute to the environment and the character of the area. There is a potential educational user but one who requires additional space which might impact on the adjoining residential areas.

Consideration therefore needs to be given as to the future of the buildings. The completed table below Figure 6.5 shows a different picture, with the building assessment revealing a much higher score. The building is valued by both the community and the potential user but it appears that in order to achieve an economic value some concessions will be needed. These are probably the benefit of planning consent for additional space but funding for repairs of the listed building might also tip the balance.

Again the matrix has been completed using a combination of factual and estimated responses. Over time, it would be possible to refine the latter with more accurate assessments to review the project. On this occasion both social and environmental indicators show that the building should be retained but the economic indicator is clearly in favour of demolition. It is therefore probable that concessions will be needed in the form of the extent of rebuilding or adaptation that will be permitted or that grant aid for the maintenance of the historic buildings may enable a positive economic assessment to be made.

The same weightings are then applied in Figure 6.6 as to the first example, again resulting in a change in response but on this occasion it increases the presumption in favour of retention.

Here there is a clear case for the retention of the building but again there is a difference in the perception of the efficiency of the site use and this may indicate a question which will have to be resolved as part of any planning application for additional space.

Thus it can be seen that the tool helps to highlight the issues concerned not only for an existing building but possibly indicating those which would need to be considered for the redevelopment of the site. The examples above

Figure 6.5: Example 2

BUILDINGS: A NEW LIFE

Tool kit
The explanation of the question headings should be read before completing the matrix.

Scoring
1 = The building performs very badly
2 = The building performs badly
3 = The building performs neither badly nor well
4 = The building performs well
5 = The building performs outstandingly well

Weighting. If the issue is particularly significant a weighting of up to three can be applied.
Sensitivity. *** indicates a considerable difference between internal and external stakeholders

Questions	External 1–5	Internal 1–5	Ext. × Int.	(E×I)/W		Sensitivity E–I
Economic						
1 Is the building efficient	3	2	6	1	6	–
2 Is there an economic return	3	2	6	1	6	–
3 Is it efficient land use	3	1	3	1	3	*
4 Form of tenure	3	4	12	1	12	–
5 Quality of transport access	3	2	6	1	6	–
6 Maintenance of fabric	2	1	2	1	2	–
7 Functional adaptability	4	1	4	1	4	**
Average figures	3.00	1.86	5.57		5.57	*
Social						
1 Cultural adaptability	5	3	15	1	15	*
2 Cultural importance	5	4	20	1	20	–
3 Lovability	4	4	16	1	16	–
4 Construction legislation	3	1	3	1	3	*
5 Occupation legislation	3	2	6	1	6	–
6 Local amenities	4	4	16	1	16	–
7 Quality of work environment	3	4	12	1	12	–
Average figures	3.86	3.14	12.57		12.57	–
Environmental						
1 Environmental standards	4	4	16	1	16	–
2 Energy – consumption	3	3	9	1	9	–
3 Energy – embodied	2	5	10	1	10	**
4 Hazardous/deleterious	3	4	12	1	12	–
5 Environmental quality	4	4	16	1	16	–
6 Ecological	2	3	6	1	6	–
7 Technological adaptability	4	4	16	1	16	–
Average figures	3.14	3.86	12.14		12.14	–
Total	**3.33**	**2.95**	**10.10**		**10.10**	

Figure 6.6: Example 2 with weighted scoring

BUILDINGS: A NEW LIFE

Tool kit
The explanation of the question headings should be read before completing the matrix.

Scoring
1 = The building performs very badly
2 = The building performs badly
3 = The building performs neither badly nor well
4 = The building performs well
5 = The building performs outstandingly well

Weighting. If the issue is particularly significant a weighting of up to three can be applied.
Sensitivity. *** indicates a considerable difference between internal and external stakeholders

Questions	External 1–5	Internal 1–5	Ext. × Int.	(E×I)/W		Sensitivity E–I
Economic						
1 Is the building efficient	3	2	6	3	18	–
2 Is there an economic return	3	2	6	3	18	–
3 Is it efficient land use	3	1	3	1	3	*
4 Form of tenure	3	4	12	1	12	–
5 Quality of transport access	3	2	6	3	18	–
6 Maintenance of fabric	2	1	2	1	2	–
7 Functional adaptability	4	1	4	3	12	**
Average figures	3.00	1.86	5.57		5.53	*
Social						
1 Cultural adaptability	5	3	15	1	15	*
2 Cultural importance	5	4	20	1	20	–
3 Lovability	4	4	16	2	32	–
4 Construction legislation	3	1	3	1	3	*
5 Occupation legislation	3	2	6	1	6	–
6 Local amenities	4	4	16	3	48	–
7 Quality of work environment	3	4	12	3	36	–
Average figures	3.86	3.14	12.57		13.33	–
Environmental						
1 Environmental standards	4	4	16	2	32	–
2 Energy – consumption	3	3	9	1	9	–
3 Energy – embodied	2	5	10	1	10	**
4 Hazardous/deleterious	3	4	12	1	12	–
5 Environmental quality	4	4	16	1	16	–
6 Ecological	2	3	6	1	6	–
7 Technological adaptability	4	4	16	3	48	–
Average figures	3.14	3.86	12.14		13.30	–
Total	**3.33**	**2.95**	**10.10**		**10.72**	

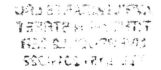

show the use of the tool to summarise the situation and in practice assembling the information to score each sector will provide a valuable source of detailed information with which to implement the decisions. The tool kit is not intended to provide an automatic decision but to focus attention on the issues to be resolved to achieve a truly sustainable building.

Key points in the use of the BSAT:

- The objective is to enable the identification of conflicts in the interests of the stakeholders so as to encourage a dialogue leading to achieving a truly sustainable environment. It is recognised that sustainability is too complex a matter to allow a simple mathematical analysis determine a buildings sustainability.
- The toolkit is designed to allow a combination of accurate appraisals and guesstimates where these are the only information available.
- Weighting can be given either to topics which are considered to be fundamental to the sustainability of the building or to those which can be more accurately assessed.
- Additional topics can be introduced either as extra questions or in place of some of those proposed in this publication. The topics suggested have been derived from the research programme which underlies the book and reflect the current interests of the cross section of respondents.
- The BSAT can also be used to assess the property for an alternative use. For instance, the two examples demonstrated are in educational use. If the buildings were adapted for conversion to, say, residential use, different scores would result.

Endnotes

1   Research shows that for the average corporation some 30–40% of the asset base is likely to be property (Currie and Scott, 1991).
2   EPC stands for energy performance coefficient.

Appendix A

The *Buildings: A New Life* Project

Introduction

Throughout the book reference is made to the research project carried out by the authors entitled *Buildings: a new life*. This project set out to inform the debate in respect of the factors that determine whether or not a building should be redeveloped or refurbished, if triple bottom line principles are adopted, as opposed to a single bottom line economic decision-making process.

This Appendix sets out, in brief, the nature of the project, its sponsors and methodology as well as outlining the main issues revealed in the investigations. The conclusions arising from the project are subsumed within the main chapters of the book.

The lead partner in the research was Professor Tony Walker, senior partner of DLG Architects and the other main partners were Professor Sarah Sayce of Kingston University and Dr Angus McIntosh of property consultants, King Sturge. The researcher for the project was Jo Koenig, then of Kingston University.

At the time that the work commenced (2000), much of the work undertaken in relation to building sustainability had focused on the construction of *new* buildings and the search for technological solutions to the *production* of so-called 'green' buildings. The emphasis was on supply factors, both in terms of materials and construction techniques.

However, the supply of new buildings accounts for probably no more than 2% of the entire stock; hence the project team took the view in promoting the work that a better understanding of the determinants of building *life* for *existing* buildings would be a contribution to the debate regarding

sustainability. The stance was adopted that longevity is *not* synonymous with sustainability but that the optimising of building life is a more appropriate goal for sustainability

The uniqueness of the *Buildings: a new life* project lay in the 'triple-bottom' line it takes to building sustainability. It started from the premise that building life is determined by a complex set of influences that combine economic, social and environmental considerations.

In developing the research the standpoint was taken that a wide range of issues affected decisions relating to the future life of a building and that these could be broadly categorised into economic, environmental and social factors – the triple bottom line (TBL). Further, from an early stage it was recognised that buildings had two sets of stakeholders: those internal to the building, such as owners and occupiers who all have a financial involvement, direct or indirect and external stakeholders, such as the community and casual users (such as shoppers and restaurant goers).

The structure of this book reflects these decisions, in that chapters have been devoted to more detailed consideration of each of the triple bottom line elements while in Chapter 2 the nature of stakeholders was discussed.

Background

The decision whether to prolong or end a building's life, be it old or relatively new, must inevitably be based on a range of factors and it is the aim of this research project to clarify these issues. Many buildings can and perhaps should be saved for the future, but the possibility of either radical change to a building's fabric or demolition must not be ruled out if a better understanding of the concept of 'sustainability' is to be achieved. The optimal solution in holistic economic, social and environmental terms may well be not to retain, but to demolish and rebuild.

In preparing the original brief, the project team recognised that a considerable amount of work had already been undertaken by many researchers looking at the sustainability of buildings in relation to forms of construction, materials used, energy use and heat loss as well as the more general physical attributes. However they considered that the search for sustainable buildings must go wider than this. The bulk of the research to date has focused on the measurable environmental issues and little attention has been given to evaluating economic and social sustainability criteria. However much design engineering provided environmentally appropriate solutions, for buildings to succeed they must do so for their owners and occupiers.

This implies economic efficiency. If a building does not meet the needs of the occupier or a class of occupier it will not have economic value and its future will be jeopardised – unless it can be brought into use for another type of occupation. Therefore the starting consideration was that the concept of economic efficiency must form a plank to the work as it recognises the link between the search for economic solutions and demand for buildings. To corporate occupiers, the buildings they occupy must be used in the most productive way possible, so it was hypothesised that the relationship between building owner and occupier as established via the commercial lease may play a key role.

The success of the building must also be measured in social terms. Far less research had taken place into these aspects as they relate to an individual building. Very few studies had measured the efficiency of a building's provision in terms of the working environment, with reference to the function of the built environment for business, the capacity of the commercial space to meet occupational requirements and the changing nature of such measurements as organisation range over time.

The project team were of the view that where such studies have taken place, they had tended to be post-occupancy evaluation of new buildings that have been designed with sustainability criteria in mind, not *post-hoc* studies of old buildings.

To date, society's response to the issue of whether or not a building 'lives' lies primarily within the hands of building owners – even though the effects of their decisions are far ranging and can affect the very grain of the urban environment. Accordingly, the decision is normally taken on purely economic grounds.

The only times when the decision (whether or not a building remains standing) does not lie with the building owner, is in the event of compulsory acquisition for public development purposes, or more commonly, if the building is listed.(1) In the case of compulsory acquisition, the decision to demolish will be taken effectively in the best community or public interests after the opportunity for debate as to the overall merits of the scheme proposal.

The research sought to explore the other factors that might – indeed should – trigger the demolition decision and to arrive at a better understanding as to how far economic considerations in fact do drive the decision making process. It was acknowledged that in seeking to influence a shift from single bottom line criteria to the triple bottom line, the findings from the project would do no more than produce some signposts along the way.

The sponsors of the project

The project was part funded by the DTI (previously DETR) under their Partners in Innovation (PII) Scheme. The remaining funding was contributed by the project partners and the organisations who made in-kind contributions by assisting in the working and advisory groups.

The personnel who constituted the main Working Group were Prof Tony Walker, Prof Sarah Sayce, Dr Angus McIntosh and Jo Koenig. Key personnel who advised and contributed their time and expertise to the project were:

John Anderson of Gateshead Borough Council,
Jerry Barford of Gateshead Borough Council,
John Doggart of ECD Consultants,
Anthony Holmes, of DLG Architects,
Hugh Seigle formerly of the Whitbread Group,
Phil Shearer of Robinson Low Francis,
Andrew Wilson of the Howard de Walden Estate

The project was overseen on behalf of the DTI (DETR) by Dr Mervyn Jones of FBE Management. In addition a large number of property and construction professionals attended Focus Group events and partook in the survey work. All influenced the Working Group members who none the less accept responsibility for the project outcomes and whose views may not be in accord with some of those involved with the consultation process.

Aims and objectives

The main ambition of the project was that the project would raise awareness of certain sustainability issues within the property and construction professions and that it would result in the production of outputs that could assist stakeholders in undertaking decisions about the future lives of buildings. It also aimed to assist in the quest for determining whether or not a building was worthy of retention, based on the premise of the TBL, that is economic, social and environmental criteria.

The principal objective of the project was to search for a better understanding of the issues that affect the useful lifespan of a commercial building. By so doing, the intention was to produce some guidance to all those charged with the design, procurement and management of buildings to move towards more sustainable buildings. This book is the result of these ambitions.

To develop the understanding and achieve the aims of the project required exploration of many complex factors, for what determines the longevity of a building was thought to be a matrix of inter-related issues. Also, throughout the conduct of the project, it was borne in mind that, whilst longevity might be a critical component of sustainability, the two are not necessarily synonymous.

Methodology

The project was undertaken in phases. These were:

- A literature review;
- Establishment of a 'matrix of issues' which was tested via a series of working and advisory group meetings;

- A questionnaire survey of groups identified as stakeholders; and
- Five case studies of different types of buildings.

In the research, the emphasis was on qualitative approaches with a literature search, workshops with invited audiences and a series of building case studies providing insights into practice. However, a quantitative survey of stakeholder groups was undertaken to confirm the key issues affecting buildings survival. This also provided very influential in the development of the key questions that are provided at the end of the relevant chapters and the key factors incorporated in the Building Sustainability Assessment Tool.

The literature review

The literature review aimed to provide a firm foundation for the work prior to consultation and fieldwork. A search was carried out in the initial stages, but it continued throughout. It aimed to establish essential tenets of this particular project in the light of earlier studies, namely that change is not necessarily desirable but may be a natural part of a building's life-cycle. The review was undertaken on the premise that buildings are, and always have been, erected with an end use in mind.

The findings from the literature review are incorporated within the book but some key messages emerged which informed the later stages of the work. These were as follows:

- A building must be **viable in the eyes of all those involved** to have come into existence and to survive from thereon (Ball *et al.*, 1998:14).
- The viability of the building depends on its **functionality**, most of all for the end user. Brand was an important influence of the findings. His work (Brand, 1997) cites the three major changes that have occurred in office space during the last 100 years: the development of the concept of office space, the use of partitions and furniture, and the last and perhaps the most crucial, the introduction of new technology.
- The **needs of the user change over time**. It follows from this that a building, which is incapable of adapting to the needs of the

Table A. 1

Section	ECI range	Ave.	ECE range	Ave.	SOI range	Ave.	SOE range	Ave	ENI range	Ave.	ENE range	Ave.
1 Culture	15–25	**18.3**	6–20	**12**	12–15	**13**	8–16	**14.6**	0–16	**6.6**	0–16	**8.3**
2 Technology	20	**20**	10–20	**14**	8–10	6.6	10–12	11.3	0–12	6	0–16	10.3
3 Building fabric	5–9	7.3	5–16	6.6	9–18	**13.6**	9–20	**15**	5–20	**13.6**	0–9	5
4 Uses	12–16	**14.3**	5–15	9	5–12	8.6	5–16	9	4–12	9.3	6–16	12.3
5 Location	12–15	**14**	9–15	**13**	15–20	**17.6**	12–15	**14**	5–20	**12.3**	4–9	6
6 Legal	4–15	10.3	4–12	6.6	2–12	7.3	3–15	10	2–8	6	0–12	4.3
7 Functionality	10–18	**14.3**	1–15	7	10–15	**13.3**	2–8	5.3	2–9	5.6	2–12	5.3
8 Re-use	6–15	10.3	1–15	9.3	12–18	**14**	4–20	**13.6**	2–15	8.6	4–12	7
9 Procurement	5–8	7	1–12	5	4–16	10.1	4–16	7.3	2–9	4.6	0–12	4.6

occupier as their requirements change, must either find a new life through adaptation either for another user within the same use type to another use.

- **If a building is not allowed to change then it will become obsolete**. References to the work of Le Corbusier spoke of buildings as functional instruments such as tools like the motorcar or typewriter and not of priceless artefacts. Again this strand picks up the requirements for buildings to have economic functionality.
- **Obsolete buildings do not survive**. In the view of Pickard (1996) when discussing the debate over the future of a number of listed buildings in Newcastle, the cause of building death is normally obsolescence, a view that can also be extracted from the work of Baum (1991). Conversely if change is allowed, then further life may occur. This promoted the idea of stakeholder dialogue. It also promoted the view of change being an inherent and natural feature of a building's life-cycle.

The matrix

A matrix was constructed in the light of initial literature work to act as a reference frame against which to test the factors thought to affect a building's continued viability. In developing this, the Working Group listed all possible influences that, in their informed opinion, could play a part in determining the chances of a building surviving.

The initially developed matrix was then scrutinised by the Advisory Group and adjusted in the light of their comments. The resultant matrix was constructed using a 'Triple Bottom Line' approach, namely accommodating economic, social and environmental concerns and was published in an interim report in 2001.

In order to recognise that, to achieve building sustainability, the interests of stakeholders who are 'external' to the building must be factored in, each heading was subdivided to produce a total of six columns as follows:

- Economic Conditions: Internal (ECI)
- Economic Conditions: External (ECE)
- Social Conditions: Internal (SOI)
- Social Conditions: External (SOE)

- Environmental Issues: Internal (ENI)
- Environmental Issues : External (ENE)

The Working Group then developed a list of issues that they considered were likely to be key issues in determining whether or not a building would continue to survive. These issues were:

- Culture
- Technology
- Building fabric
- Building use
- Location
- Legal
- Functionality
- Re-use
- Procurement

The result was a matrix of 54 different considerations (nine issues and six sustainability factors). Each member of the Working and Advisory Group then completed the matrix using a scoring system.

For each of the 54 cells each member scored the likely affect from a maximum of 25 to a minimum of zero. The results were then collated and the results are shown on the grid (Table A. 1).

Although there was a wide variation in the individual scores attributed, due in no small part to the differing individual perspectives of the Team members, it was possible to identify certain key items that scored highly. These have been emboldened in the grid and the top 15 factors as revealed by the matrix are considered below. The results were considered only in terms of their mean scores not their standard deviation, given the small numbers of people who contributed to this exercise. It is instantly noticeable that environmental issues were scored more lowly than either economic or social factors. Taking a cross sectional approach, locational issues were important under all three headings, whereas culture and functionality were important economically and socially – but not in environmental terms.

The common themes that emerged are summarised below:

- The ability to change and adapt was considered paramount, both in relation to the economic context and to working practices.
- Environmental and technology issues were very low in terms of importance to prolonging building life.

- Location and context of the building is very important to all stakeholders, both internal and external.
- The 'heritage' value and the extent to which a building is considered to add to the urban fabric were also considered to be important.

Developing these key findings in the light of the Working and Advisory Group meetings reveals the following, in order of ranking.

1   *Building allows new ways of working with technology (technology internal) and ability to constrain maintenance and running costs (ECI).* This result echoes the need that a building must be capable of adapting to new ways of working. If it does not functional obsolescence will set in. With the progressive introduction of energy use taxation the issue of running costs will possibly become more critical.

2   *Ability to change to high value economy with different workplace needs and to accommodate international links (ECI).* This factor underlines the need to relate to changing economic conditions. A building, which is capable of being in high value use and if necessary adaptation to continue in high value use is very important. For example, with the rise of eating out the rents that many restaurant units can command often show a premium over straight retail. A building that physically has the attributes to change to accommodate this trend will be more likely to live.

3   *Working relationships with other companies or associates and access for clients and customers can be accommodated (SOI).* The old adage of location is a powerful one. The nature of locational advantage may change; buildings, which are perceived to offer long-term location advantage, may be more likely to live.

4   *The heritage value of this building is important (SOE).* Heritage value, or the ability to add to the ambience of the environment was the most highly rated of all external factors as it affects whether external stakeholders place the building in high regard. This factor is closely linked to the arguments for listing, except in so far as this factor may recognise the setting of the building as much as the building itself.

5   *The impact of new activities, such as the growth of café society, can be accommodated (SOE).* Over time, the demands society places on buildings change; this factor recognises this and relates as the external face of the internal economic expression shown in 1 above.

6   *The building form or areas supports an economic way of working; the building form is adaptable to new uses and ways of working (ECI).* This factor again relates to 1 above but relates specifically to the building form and matters such as inherent flexibility.

7   *The building has suitability for alternate economic uses (ECI).* This again relates to flexible form and the ability for a building owner or occupier to recognise the potential to change the use as economic and social circumstances change.

8   *The building provides a relationship with other activities in the immediate environment in a balanced economy, including transport and access (SOE).* In this factor the context within which the building fits was considered. Does it relate to other buildings and its market? It was considered that an isolated building with little contextual relationship would be less likely to survive.

9   *The building is located such that it is appropriate in terms of the cost of transport for goods, staff or customers (ECI).* This is an economic consideration. Without accessibility to markets and labour force, a building will not retain economic value.

10 *The building is located such that it relates to other activities (including access) such that a balanced economy can be achieved (SOE).* This factor relates to location in terms of an appropriate setting for occupiers and employees in terms of social and transport infrastructure.

11 *The building is capable of being marketed for re-use opportunities (SOI).* This factor, although listed under social factors relates very closely to the economic. If it is not capable of being so-marketed by implication is it due to a lack of economic value in re-use

12 *The building is capable of adapting to different working patterns (SOI).* This factor related solely to the ability of the fabric of the building to accommodate different working practices –

such as the moves to or from cellular layout of offices.

13 *The building is built with historic materials that have associations with re-use (SOE).* This factor examined the ability of traditional materials to be re-usable – for example the durability in performance terms of say wood compared with plastic.

14 *The building is fashionable in appearance and is capable of changes in perceived needs such as changing illumination levels (ENI).* This was listed as environmental fabric issues hence tying the response to technological not aesthetic responses.

15 *The quality of the environment of the building is important in terms of being loveable and likeable (SOI).* In some ways it was surprising that this ranked so low, and may have been an issue of interpretation as to whether the 'environment' was to mean the building envelope or the surroundings.

In further considering these findings some interesting themes emerged. The matrix allowed for 54 characteristics to be evaluated, one third being economic, a third being social and the last third being environmental. Of the top 15 factors identified by the working group:

- 5 were economic
- 9 were social, and
- 1 only was environmental.

However, if only the top 10 factors are considered a very different picture emerges: a 50/50 split between economic and social factors. Out of the top 15, 10 are internal to the building, giving the 'internal' stakeholder control in most cases, and five relate to the building in its wider setting.

Cutting the matrix along its other axis, of the nine factors (culture, technology etc.) the findings were less polarised as follows:

- Location: 3
- Building Fabric: 3
- Technology: 2
- Culture: 2
- Functionality: 2
- Re-usability: 2
- User: 1

It was noted that legal and procurement factors did not feature.

Drawing these strands together indicated that issues such as energy efficiency were deemed to be less important (taking a long-term perspective) than issues such as location and the essential nature of the building fabric, and its ability to provide a social environment that meets the requirements of its occupier.

The findings of the matrix exercise confirmed the review of current opinion in a number of respects: the predominance of concerns **internal** to the building reflects the need for **economic** viability on the eyes of the user, and underlines the fact that **obsolete** buildings stand a slimmer chance of survival.

However, what was not predicted was the importance that was given to the surroundings and location in a 'social' or contextual framework could militate for or against a building's chances of survival. The matrix also revealed some strongly divergent views.

The questionnaire survey

Accordingly, to gain a wider perspective, a questionnaire was developed and sent out with a covering letter in December 2000 to 600 individuals covering a wide geographic area of the UK representing four key stakeholder groups. The matrix was not used as it was considered to complex a tool to use for a postal survey.

The aim was to ascertain whether there was general support for the opinions put forward by the Working Group in the matrix, as confirmed by the Advisory Group. The postal questionnaire contained 31 questions relating to survivability of a building. Four main stakeholder groups were targeted:

- Architects and designers; the key proponents in the decision process;
- Property companies and developers;
- Planners, acting as surrogates for the community stakeholders; and
- Businesses and occupiers, to give the user perspective.

From the postal questionnaire survey a response rate of 19.5% was received. Of 116 questionnaires returned, the break down was as follows.

Designers and Architects	25
Local Authority Planners	49

Table A.2: Ranking according to the questionnaire survey (N.B 1 is the highest rank, 31 the lowest)

Average Rank	Question	Planners	Architects	Businesses	Developers
1	Does the long term durability of the building fabric have a significant effect on the survival of the building?	2	4	3	1
2	To what degree is it important for survival that a building adapts to reflect the changing needs of the user?	3	3	1	2
3	To what extent do you consider that the buildings ability to be used in an economical way may effect survival?	1	2	2	3
4	To what extent does listed building and/or conservation area legislation affect the survival of a building?	4	1	12	4
5	Does the ability of the building to adapt to new technology requirements affect its survival?	5	5	6	5
6	Does the internal environmental standard of light, heat, air quality, noise affect the survival of a building?	12	9	4	10
7	Does the presence of new technology affect survival by delivering a satisfactory environment and/or functional building?	10	10	5	9
8	Does the use of specialised components raise problems for the long term maintenance and survival of a building?	9	7	11	6
9	To what extent do planning constraints affect the survival of a building?	6	19	6	16
10	Does the quality of the immediate environment effect the buildings chance of survival?	7	8	15	13
11	To what extent does the building survival depend upon the degree to which it is liked by its user?	13	18	13	12
12	Does the internal layout of the circulation of service areas of a building have affect on the survival of that building?	19	6	18	8
13	Does the building form (tall small floorplates, low wide plan, large open space, or small circular space, etc) affect the survival of the building?	22	12	9	19
14	Does the range of amenities in a locality affect survival?	11	24	16	7
15	Does the availability of car parking space affect the survival of the building?	27	11	8	22
16	A configuration of a building does not meet emerging business/activities structures, i.e. hot desking, homeworking, flexi hours, a 24 hour society	26	23	10	14
17	Does the quality of public transport effect the long term survival of a building?	8	29	14	23
18	Does the increasing pace of technological change affect the sustainability of the building?	25	15	17	18
19	Is the survival of a building affected by fashion and appearance and perception of viability of use by its user?	23	20	20	17
20	How is the survival of a building affected by the decision to put it to a use that ensures that the fabric's durability, rather than meeting the needs of a community?	20	13	22	28
21	To what degree is it important for the survival that a building adapts to reflect the changing needs of the community?	18	14	23	30

Table A.2: continued

Average Rank	Question	Planners	Architects	Businesses	Developers
22	Does the use of traditional materials result in benefits for the sustainability of the community, through the creation of local employment for maintenance/alteration?	14	22	30	15
23	Does the use of traditional materials affect the long term survival of the building?	21	16	31	11
24	Does the use of 'green' or 'natural' means of environmental control effect the survival of the building?	16	21	25	29
25	To what extent does workplace legislation affect a building's survival?	15	25	26	21
26	To what extent does a building's survival depend on the degree to what it is liked by the community?	24	26	24	25
27	Does the complexity of environmental control systems affect the survival of the building?	28	30	19	31
28	Does ease of access for disabled or disadvantaged persons affect the building's chance of survival?	17	31	28	24
29	Does fashion in planning types of workspace affect the long term survival of a building?	29	17	29	27
30	Does the use of system building with interchangeable components enhance the chances of survival of the building?	31	28	21	26
31	Is the survival of a building affected by fashions in appearance and perception or viability of use by the community?	30	27	27	30

Businesses and Occupiers	22
Property Companies/Developers	20
Total	116

The responses to this questionnaire survey provided further clarification as to the important issues in terms of building sustainability. The table also shows the ranking according to whether the questionnaire was received from Local Authority Planners, Designers and Architects, Business and Occupiers or Property Company Developers. These demonstrated some important differences between these four different sectors of the commercial property market. Table A.2 sets out the questions and the responses.

Analysis of the questionnaire results

From the tabulated results in Table A.2 it can be seen that the durability of the fabric, which had perhaps been 'taken as read' by those completing the matrix, was considered to be the most important item overall. Adaptability to the user's needs was on average ranked second but occupier respondents felt that it was the most important feature, thus backing Brand's assertion that buildings need to 'learn' to adapt to changing needs (Brand, 1997). Adaptability to IT and other technological advance was also highly rated.

The building's setting and legal constraints rank highly among the factors deemed to affect building life, with conservation area status, listing and the quality of the immediate environment all ranking within the top 10 issues. For planners, who were taken to be a close surrogate for the community interest, the perception is that the ability to use a building economically is the most important issue. Equally important in understanding the issue of building's sustainability, is to understand what is *not* important.

For ease of the reader the five most important and least important issues are tabulated below (Table A.3 and Table A.4).

Table A.3: Top five issues considered most important in promoting longevity

Rank	Question
1	The building has a long term durable fabric.
2	The building is capable of adaptation to reflect the changing needs of the user.
3	The building is capable of being used in an economical way.
4	The location of the building is within a conservation area or is listed.
5	The building is able to be adapted to new technology requirements.

Table A.4: Top five issues considered least important in promoting longevity

Rank	Question
27	The complexity of environmental control systems affects the survival of the building.
28	The ease of access for disabled or disadvantaged persons affects the building's chance of survival.
29	Fashion in planning types of workspace affects the long-term survival of a building.
30	The use of system building with interchangeable components enhance the chances of survival of the building.
31	Fashions in appearance and perception or viability of use by the community affects building survival.

It can also be observed that for some issues there was considerable consensus between respondents, but some issues produced wide disagreement between the groups, mirroring the divergence observed in the matrix exercise. Table A.5 shows the areas over which opinion was most divers.

Table A.5: Issues over which differing views were expressed

Rank Range	Question
6–19	Planning constraints affect the survival of a building.
7–24	The range of amenities in a locality affects survival.
8–27	The availability of car parking space affects the survival of the building.
8–29	Public transport availability affects survival.
9–22	Building form affects the survival of the building.

The questionnaire and matrix results compared

The questionnaire findings supported those of the matrix in that to no stakeholder groups were the issues of 'green construction' and matters to do with promoting user welfare (such as workplace legislation) regarded as very important. Again, as with the matrix some quite marked differences in view were expressed between groups with differing perspectives. These were in each case fairly predictable in that, to planners, matters such as amenities including public transport were important, while to business occupiers issues such as car parking were more likely to feature.

Unlike the matrix, the answers enable only a simple ranking to be determined – there was no weighting system incorporated. In interpreting the findings, for each of the items listed, an attempt was been made to categorise them into the same six heads of sustainability as were used for detailing the matrix results.

1. Long-term durability of building's fabric (ENI)
It is clear that the durability of a building's fabric is important to the survival of a building over time. It is also evident that a number of buildings have lasted many centuries or even many millennia, as a result of the quality of the fabric. Some buildings from the Egyptian or the Classical world are obvious examples. This point the Working Group had effectively 'taken as read' and it was not surprising that the survey respondents ranked as important

the basic ability of the building to stand over time. Interestingly, although it achieved an overall top rank, architects had placed it at number 4!

2. *Ability to adapt to changing needs of the user (ECI)*

The second most important issue is a changing need of a user. If a building cannot adapt to such changing needs, it is not likely to survive over time. The issue raised by this question is: how do we judge changing needs, or how to design building such that they can be adapted over time. For instance, office buildings can normally, in structural terms, be turned into housing or housing being turned into office use (but not always). However, other buildings have less flexible envelopes by their very nature and are therefore more susceptible to *economic* obsolescence. For example, although the cinema of the 'thirties' may have found a re-use as a bingo hall in the 'sixties' and as a public house at the turn of the Millennium, the mothballed multiplex cinema presents a current challenge. Perhaps not surprisingly businesses ranked this as their chief concern. They require fitness for purpose.

3. *Ability to use in an economical way (ECI)*

The issue ranked third is the building's ability to be used in an economic way over time. Although this relates to changing needs as above, it clearly has financial implications. It raises the issue as to 'who pays' if a building is to survive over time. This links to questions of building efficiency in terms of energy, layout, etc., but given that the overall costs of building occupation are primarily related to the economic factors such as rental level this factor is ranked as one affecting economic, not environmental, sustainability.

4. *Building listed or in a conservation area (SOE)*

This is the first question that creates a major difference in view between respondent groups. Whilst planners, architects and developers believe this is important to a building survival, business occupiers do not see this as important; they rank it only 12th, not in the top 4! This factor relates to the legal environment and is, in effect, a measure of the community response to the area. To those whose professional lives are linked to the practicalities of the property life cycle, the impact of listing is critical. Not only does listing normally ensure that the fabric

remains, even if there is no longer economic purpose, but it can in some cases enhance value, thus supporting the viability of the building.

5. *Building's ability to adapt to technological changes (ECI)*

There is general agreement that this is an important issue, and relates to the concept of changing needs and economic use, as mentioned above. The spate of demolitions of inflexible concrete framed post-war buildings, which could not adapt to the needs of the 1980s requirement for cabling adds evidence to support this view. There was no real variation between respondent groups.

6. *Internal environmental standard of heat light air quality and noise (ENI)*

Both this contention and the one listed in 7th place were more highly ranked (4th) by businesses than other respondents, who did not place the issue within their chief concerns. The results point to a strong message for all those concerns with the development of new commercial stock: occupiers do have strong views on the standards they require in terms of the buildings they occupy.

7. *Presence of new technology delivers better working environment (ENI)*

Once again, there is a major difference in the views expressed by different respondent groups. Business occupiers see a building's ability to adapt a new technology as being important to its survival. However, planners, architects and property developers see this as less important. This highlights once again the issue of 'who pays'. If the business occupier is paying for a building's survival, it must be adaptable to new technology, as the presence of up to date technology is necessary to ensure continued usefulness.

8. *Use of specialised components (ENI)*

Property Developers clearly think that the use of specialist components does raise problems for the long term maintenance and survival of a building. They are worried about unnecessary costs and problems over time. However, Business Occupiers have not identified this as being quite so important and rank it only 11th.

9. *Planning Issues (SOE)*

The overall rank of 9th was perhaps lower than might have been expected and showed a difference of view between respondents. Interestingly both architects and property developers do not think that planning constraints affect the long-term survival of a building – maybe suggesting a confidence that, barring listing, any planning difficulties in achieving a redevelopment can and will be overcome. However, planners (who issue such planning constraints) and business occupiers think this will affect a building's ability to survive over time.

10. *Quality of immediate environment (SOE)*
Once again, there is a major polarisation with business occupiers and property developers not believing this to be very important. However, planners and architects place the item within their 'top ten'. Given that the quality of the environment can have such a significant *value* effect on a building, the working group found this result quite surprising and will test it through the case study work.

11. *Liked by user (SOI)*
It has been contended that one of the tests of the sustainability of a building is its 'likeability', yet no group rated this factor highly. Perhaps it could be questioned as it what respondents imputed by this question. Certainly buildings do evoke emotional responses – but the view of respondents is that a quality of likeability will not be enough to ensures longevity – if it is economically not appropriate.

12. *Internal layout of circulation and service area (ENI)*
The responses to this question brought a sharp divide between respondents. Those involved with the conception of a building directly (architects and developers) rated these issues as important as they do indeed affect 'lettability' and value. However, once occupied the matter seems to not be regarded as critical to the occupiers. The planners on this occasion shared views with the business occupiers.

13. *Building form (ECI)*
The factors that all agreed were the most important relate to the ability to adapt a building to ensure that it continues to meet the economic needs of the occupiers. To the businesses it appears that they relate matters of building form to their use of the building. To the other respondent groups it appears to be of little importance – possibly because they view the subject from a wider

perspective and consider within their responses the possibility of change of use (for example, industrial to leisure), which would not necessarily be within the contemplation of business occupiers who take a mono-use perspective.

14. *Range of amenities in the locality (SOE)*
In the view of architectures this issue was one of the least important (24th out of 31 issues tested). Does this suggest that architects view buildings as individual statements – rather than integral parts of the urban grain? To the developers, who need to promote a building within its context for marketing purposes and to them the presence of local amenities, such as leisure and retail facilities for office workers can enhance both rental and yield levels and ensure sustained economic returns.

15. *Availability of car parking spaces (SOI)*
Divergent views were expressed here. To businesses a car dependency culture is evident, with the presence of car parking ranked within the top ten issues! Once again, the question of 'who pays' arose. If a Business Occupier cannot obtain car spaces, he is less likely to use that particular building. Planners, maybe in promotion of green travel plans do not rate car parking as a matter that will affect building longevity and rank it almost at the bottom of their list (27th out of 31).

In summary, the survey pointed to all three elements of the bottom line (economic, social and environmental) as having an important role in determining the ability of a building to survive over time. If only the top five issues were taken, it was the economic factors that dominated.

The survey also demonstrated very clearly that the views of different stakeholder groups could be extremely divergent: what the planners, with their community role, may wish to see will be at variance in many cases with the needs of the occupier. Yet, unless such differences can be reconciled, decision making will be dominated by the power of the single bottom line – without due consideration of longer term sustainability objectives.

The case studies

To complement the work undertaken via the matrix and survey, a study of five case studies was undertaken during 2001 to test whether the factors revealed by the research held in practice and to ascertain rich information. The buildings chosen were of different ages, structural form, current uses and location; in short they were deliberately diverse. They included one that failed and was due for demolition, as well as others that have survived in areas where surrounding buildings have not. The ages of the selected buildings range from a warehouse constructed some 200 years ago to a post-war office building. The choice was also constrained in part by the need to investigate longitudinal information.

It was recognised that such a small number of case studies would not yield statistically valid findings. However it was hoped that they would provide insightful information; this proved to be the case. The buildings that were studied were:

- The Rodboro Building, Guildford
- The Old Town Hall, Gateshead
- Warehouses 1 & 2, West India Dock, London
- 141 Euston Road, London
- The Astoria Cinema, Ashford, Surrey

For reasons of confidentiality, the case studies cannot be detailed. A short description of each is provided, together with the reasons for its choice as a building to study. After the descriptions a summary of the some of the main learning points is provided.

The Rodboro Buildings, Guildford

The Rodboro Building is situated in the middle of Guildford, Surrey, which is a prosperous county town within easy commuting distance of London. Although the building is physically close to both the main shopping precinct (The Friary Centre) and the railway station it is isolated from the retail by a major gyratory system which was constructed since the early 1970s. The site also connects to an area that was, for many years, dominated by civic uses (such as the Law Courts, public swimming pool and car parking) but which has changed character in the last two decades with the development of a number of offices close to the railway station and a multiplex cinema.

The building was chosen for analysis as it provides an example of a property that is sur-rounded by buildings that have been redeveloped; it has gone through a period during which it lost economic life, lay empty and was at risk of demolition. The detailed investigations, though not chronicled here, provided rich information as to factors that helped determine its future.

The building was constructed on ground with two floors over at the beginning of the 20th century and it was the first assembly line car production plant in England. It is primarily for this historical interest that it was listed Grade II in the 1980s, although its architectural merit was also a factor in the decision. It soon outgrew its original use and was converted, first into a car showroom, but later it was used as retail with offices over.

The construction of the new road system led to the building, and others close by, falling into dis-use and it was subsequently acquired by the local authority, just prior to listing. Although there were attempts to obtain listed building consent for its demolition for further road widening schemes, these were unsuccessful, partly due to the reaction of local people to the prospect of demolition and the building was retained. At that time commercial re-use would not have been economically viable.

Guildford Borough Council had intentions to turn the Rodboro Building into an art gallery but public funds were not available. The building remained vacant for many years and eventually there was a change of heart, and once again it acquired a commercial use. The building's sustainability was determined by conversion from a wealth creating to a wealth consuming building and could have survived due to public finance, but change of use to a commercial form of wealth consumption building saved it from dereliction. The significance of the comparison between these building categories was not identified by the matrix or questionnaire but emerged as a result of the case study assessments.

It was only in the mid 1990s, during a period of economic growth and social change which resulted in the growth of the bar and restaurant trade, that it once more found a life and was converted to a large public house, trading as J D Wetherspoons and the upper parts were converted for use as a music school and studio. At the time of writing these uses continue and the adjoining locale has been re-vitalised into a 'leisure quarter'.

The Old Town Hall, Gateshead

The Old Town Hall, Gateshead, was designed by John Johnstone and built in 1870 for civic purposes. It is situated near the banks of the Tyne at a busy road junction and close to the main bridge to Newcastle. The area where it stands was once a residential street with properties dating from the period of 19th century industrial expansion, but the residential use has mainly been lost, replaced by civic buildings.

The town of Gateshead owed its wealth originally to the heavy industries of the 19th century but, despite post-war redevelopment, the town has struggled economically, but is again undergoing a revival with several regeneration initiatives, such as the Norman Foster designed concert centre.

The reasons for including the Old Town Hall in the study are that it represents an owner occupied landmark building that was constructed, not for financial return but as an expression of civic pride and responsibility as well as to serve the needs of a then prosperous town. At the time of investigation, the future life had not been resolved, so it presented an opportunity to observe decision-making in action regarding a building without proven occupational demand.

The building was used as a Town Hall with ancillary community purposes until 1988 when the council offices were relocated. The ancillary purposes included acting as a courthouse, concert hall/theatre, and it even has a lock-up in the cellar. In 1986 the building was listed (Grade II) on the grounds of its architectural merit. Despite the listing, which would make redevelopment difficult, if not impossible, the council moved out into more modern offices nearby, although they continued to use part of the building for their computing services. Even this use had stopped by the time of investigation and the building was standing empty, although the council was investigating possible re-use for their own purposes. There were no published plans to attempt to demolish the building or part with it; instead the intention was to find a new life for it.

Warehouses 1 & 2, West India Dock Road, London

Warehouses 1 & 2, West India Dock Road are situated in the heart of London's now booming docklands. However in the midst of the modern high rise development, they remain – structurally, if not by use – a reminder of a past economic era. They were chosen for study for just this reason: as an example of buildings that had 'missed the development boat' but found economic viability through adaptation and change of use.

They were constructed as part of the West India dock development at the beginning of the 19th century, at a time when London was growing fast as an international port. These docks were the first, and arguably the finest walled docks to be built. The buildings themselves are five-storey high constructed in traditional load bearing brickwork.

By the 1960s the Port of London was declining in importance and the docks were no longer capable of handling the large vessels required for containerised goods. By 1973 the dockland area was the subject of a major report as to future options in the light of decreasing viability. So started a period of uncertainty, during which the port of London Authority sought to redevelop the properties. However, consent was refused and Warehouses 1 & 2 were listed as being of historic importance.

By 1981, the docks were finally closed and the government set up the London Docklands Development Corporation (LDDC) and tasked it with the regeneration of the area. This involved large sums of public money or tax allowances and it is through this form of public subsidy that the viability of private sector investment was achieved. The LDCC had the power to override planning decisions by the local borough but, although many of the surrounding buildings were demolished, these buildings were not. They continued to lie empty and derelict until the economic revival of the area, following large-scale office redevelopment at the adjoining Canary Wharf, increased residential values, such that conversion to their present use of residential units achieved financial viability.

141 Euston Road, London

141 Euston Road comprises a hotel and residential development situated in an area of mixed uses in central London. The predominant surrounding use is office, but there are a large number of residential units and the whole area is within a very short distance of Euston mainline station.

The building was included for study as, like some of the other units, it has survived when many other examples of similar buildings within close proximity have failed. However, unlike the other case studies of buildings that have survived seemingly against the odds. 141 Euston Road is not listed as of architectural or historic interest. It therefore had no statutory protection to help ensure its longevity.

The site on which the present building sits was first developed in the 18th century as central London developed northwards, but the present building dates from the mid 1960s and is the most modern of the those studied.

The original buildings on the site were terraced houses with some industrial and office use, but there had been considerable war damage. The current building was developed by Laings and comprises in part a five-storey block and in part a 10-storey tower. The building had planning consent for offices and 32 flats and the requirement was that the residential units should be used for social housing. On part of the ground floor, at the east of the development is a petrol filling station. The building was sold to a developer on completion and the whole was let to the local authority, who sub-let both the flats and offices.

During the 1980s many of the surrounding buildings were redeveloped during the office boom of the period. However, the office parts of the building, which did not meet then modern specifications, increasingly fell vacant as it failed to meet occupier requirements. By the early 1990s, as the London office suffered a glut of space, the office space lay empty. The combination of the con-figuration of the building, the requirement to retain the residential units for social housing, the poor returns then available on office developments, led to the building remaining empty. It was some while later that it found a new life by conversion to a budget hotel, for which its location and floor plate size rendered it very suitable. Such a use was also compatible with the requirements of the local development plan. It opened as a Travel Inn in 1996 and has continued trading as such until the present time, incorporating the petrol filling station some time later. Meanwhile the residential use continues.

The Astoria Cinema, Church Street, Ashford, Middlesex

The Astoria Cinema was developed in 1938. It was constructed in art deco form and, unlike many

cinemas of its time, it had the benefit of a car park to the rear. It was located in the centre of a small settlement that lies within the Middlesex/Surrey border commuter belt on the banks of the River Thames.

As a settlement, Ashford has not developed commercially to any significant extent, being overshadowed by neighbouring Staines. It has retained an essentially residential small-town characteristic.

The building was chosen as it represented one that, despite being of a user type for which there was, at the time of the study, a buoyant market, was failing. Many cinemas of this age have found a new life as public houses, restaurants or other leisure venues. This property was one that was due for demolition and replacement with sheltered housing.

The property operated as a cinema until the mid 1970s when the national decline in cinema admissions finally forced the operators, Rank, to close it, despite documented complaints from local residents who did not wish to see the loss of a local entertainment venue. However, it was converted to a Bingo Hall and operated as such by Mecca for a period of approximately ten years, when this too ceased. Since that time the building has stood empty, with further uses proving either to lack financial viability or to go against existing restrictive covenants placed on the building. In 2001, at the time of this investigation, consent had just been granted for its demolition and replacement by sheltered housing.

Key points emerging from the case studies

A number of key points arose from the case studies that augmented and in some cases challenged the relative significance of the findings of the previous two phases. They were

Building flexibility and adaptability

The buildings chosen for study had all faced risk of demolition; most had survived, but in every case this was related to a change of use. Without this ability, they would probably have all failed, despite listing. Therefore building flexibility is found to be probably the single most critical factor. However, the definition of flexibility is broad. For the case study buildings what was critical was *adaptability* – especially across use. The ability to change use is a common factor for survival but will need to reflect the demands of market trends. The only exception was the Old Town Hall, Gateshead which never came under the same development pressures – but which at the date of investigation had not found a new life and was only being kept from pressure to demolish by the attitudes of its internal stakeholders.

Energy efficiency and costs in use

The results from the working group matrix exercise and of the survey had revealed that matters such as energy efficiency were not regarded as highly important to building longevity. Instead the overall economic aspects and its *adaptability* are far more important. This was indeed borne out in the case studies, where issues of costs in use and energy were not significant considerations within the decision-making process.

Loveability

The case studies demonstrated that the attitudes of local residents could be influential. Quite apart from the matter of statutory listing, the case studies revealed, through examination of newspapers and planning records, that the influence of local people formed important influences on those with decision-making powers. The extent to which a building has 'loveability' qualities recognised by its external stakeholders can be an important element is establishing its sustainability profile. It is notable that some millennium and lottery funded projects, which it may be assumed reflected support and engagement by the local community, have failed due to the need to create an adequate business case. Loveability alone is not enough.

Legal and planning constraints

Legal constraints on a building in the form of restrictive covenants or/and onerous lease terms, were issues that arose in more than one of the case studies. Whilst such issues can be damaging to the financial interests of some of the internal stakeholders, they can be influential in determining the viability (or otherwise) of development at times

when a building's future is in doubt. Potentially, flexible leases, as currently advocated, might lead to shorter building lives, as they would make possession easier to obtain at times when profits to be obtained through redevelopment. Overall the effects of legal matters were found to be more influential in the case studies that had been revealed by either the matrix or survey.

Changes of use proved critical in almost every case. For the three buildings whose futures now appear most secure, it was a change of use from wealth-creation (i.e. industrial or office) to wealth-spending uses (residential or leisure) that has been critical. For this to take place the structure must be such that *adaptability across use* is possible – and the social context must be appropriate.

Literature had suggested that commercial buildings once listed have a mixed record in terms of their sustainability and a key to building survival lies more in its ability to change over time. From the case studies, the presence of listing was found to be influential in preventing the loss of buildings at times of economic decline. However, this was not the whole story; survival is not assured by listing – it was the regaining of economic life that is critical. The attitude of the owner is also a key consideration

Functionality and the economic cycle

The research has demonstrated throughout the importance of occupier demand or current utility of a building in ensuring its survival. A building without an economic use to its internal stakeholders cannot be regarded as sustainable. However conversely, the case studies demonstrate that sometimes, a *lack* of economic value can mean that a building is simply not worth demolishing. Then with social and economic change, especially if there is public finance (such as Guildford Borough Council purchasing the Rodboro Buildings) or lottery finance, it may find a new life – one that would not have occurred had it come to a 'break point' at a time of high economic activity.

From the case studies evidence was found that if parties are willing to wait, successful solutions can be found but only when market forces once more become accommodating. This is more likely in the case of an owner-occupied building. Consequently it is suggested that interaction of economic context to 'pressure points' (such as ownership change) may be vital. It is suggested from the experience of the case study buildings that listing, by itself, does not provide 'a new life' – but a possible 'breathing space' until such time as the economic and locational context changes.

Overall, the case studies provided the Research Team with a rich set of data from which to further refine their thinking and inform the contents of this book and in particular, the development of the Building Sustainability Assessment Tool.

Endnote

1   In making this contention it is accepted that in many cases a building owner may be prevented from demolishing due to the presence of other legal or statutory interests in the building, for example through leases, easements etc.

Appendix B

Glossary

BPF	British Property Federation
BRE	Building Research Establishment
BREEAM	Building Research Establishment Environmental Assessment Method
BSAT	Building Sustainability Assessment Tool
CARM	Centre for Advanced and Renewable Materials
CBI	Confederation of British Industry
CFC	Chlorofluorocarbons
CH_4	Methane
CO_2	Carbon Dioxide
CSR	Corporate Social Responsibility
DETR	Department of the Environment Transport and the Regions
DJSI	Dow Jones Sustainability Index
DoE	Department of the Environment
DTI	Department of Trade and Industry
EPC	Energy Performance Coefficient
EU	European Union
FCA	Full Cost Accounting
GDP	Gross Domestic Product
Gj	Gigajoules
HERS	Home Energy Rating Scheme
HMSO	Her Majesty's Stationery Office
ILO	International Labour Organisation
IPD	Investment Property Databank
Kg	Kilogram
Km	Kilometre
KPI	Key Performance Indicators
M^2	Metre squared
Mj	Mega joules
N_2O	Nitrous Oxide
NACORE	National Association of Corporate Real Estate Executives
NIC	National Insurance Contribution
OECD	Organisation for Economic Co-operation and Development
QoL	Quality of Life
RIBA	Royal Institution of British Architects
RICS	Royal Institution of Chartered Surveyors
RTPI	Royal Town Planning Institute
SAP	Standard Assessment Procedure
SRI	Socially Responsible Investment
TBL	Triple Bottom Line
UAE	United Arab Emirates
UDP	Unitary Development Plan
UK	United Kingdom
UN	United Nations
USA	United States of America
VDU	Visual Display Unit
VOC	Volatile Organic Compound
WCED	World Commission on Environment and Development

Appendix C

References and Selected Further Reading

Chapter 1

Baum A (1991) *Property Investment Depreciation and Obsolescence* London: International Thomson Business Press

Baum A (1994) Quality and property performance *Journal of Property Valuation and Investment* 12 (1) 31–46

Baum A and McElhinney (2001) *The Causes and Effects of Depreciation in Office Buildings, A ten year update* Working Papers in Land Management and Development 07/00: University of Reading

Bell S and Morse S (1999) *Sustainability Indicators* London: Earthscan

Brand S (1997) *How Buildings Learn* 2nd Ed. London: Phoenix Illustrated

Building Research Establishment [BRE] (2000) *Green Guide to Building Specification* Garston: BRE

Department of the Environment Transport and the Regions (1999) Disability Discrimination Act London: HMSO

Edwards B (2001) *Green Architecture – An International Comparison* London: John Wiley & Sons

European Construction Industry Federation (2000) The FIEC Charter *A European building efficiency for the environment and jobs*

Howard N (1996) Embodied Energy and Consequential CO_2 in Construction *Proceedings of the 1996 International Symposium of CIBW67 on Energy and Massblown Buildings* Vienna: August

Kincaid D (2002) *Adapting Buildings for Changing Uses* London: E&FN Spon Press

Lovett I (2001) *Green today, gone tomorrow* Kingston University: Unpublished MSc Thesis

Morpeth N (2003) Local implementation structures and the operationalisation of the principles of sustainability *Proceedings of the International Sustainable Development Research Conference* Shipley Yorkshire: ERP Publications

Morse S (2002) Towards a Sustainable Development Index *Proceedings of the Annual International Sustainable Development Research Conference* Shipley Yorkshire: ERP Publications

Rashleigh B (2000) Green Strategy to cut CO_2 Building Design *Building Design* 13 October, p6

Rogers R (1999) *Towards an Urban Renaissance: The Report of the Urban Task Force* London: E&FN Spon

Sayce S, Parnell P, Iball H (2001) *The Business Case for Sustainable Property* Draft final report to the Construction Confederation

Thomas R (1999) *Environmental Design* 2nd Ed London: E&FN Spon

Williamson T, Radford A, Bennets H (2003) *Understanding Sustainable Architecture* London: E&FNSpon

World Commission on Environment and Development (1987) *Our Common Future* Oxford: Oxford University Press

www.carillionplc.com

www.cbpp.org.uk

www.ftse4good.com

www.sloughestates.com

www.sustainability-index.com

www.un.org

Chapter 2

Bebbington J, Gray R, Hibbitt C, Kirk E (2001) *Full Cost Accounting: an agenda for action* London: Association of Chartered Certified Accountants

Brookings Institute (2002) *Corporate Social Responsibility: Partners for Progress* Washington DC: US Brookings Institute

Coleman AM (1985) *Utopia on Trial: vision and reality in planned housing* London: Hilary Shipman Ltd

Cooper MC, Sarkissian W (1986) *Housing as if People Mattered* California: University of California Press Berkeley

Freeman RE (1994) *Strategic Management: A stakeholder approach* Boston: Pitman/ Ballinger

Heertz N (2000) *The Silent Takeover: Global Capitalism and the Death of Democracy* London: Heinneman

Hopkins M (2003) *The Planetary Bargain: Corporate Social Responsibility Matters* London: Earthscan Publications Ltd

Kaplan S, Kaplan R (1982) *Humanscape, Environments for People* Michigan: Ulrich Ann Arbor

Klein N (2001) *No Logo* London: Flamingo

Lovelock JE (1979) *Gaia: A New Look at Life on Earth* Oxford: Oxford University Press

Margolis JD, Walsh JP (2001) *People and Profits? The Search for a Link Between a Company's Social and Financial Performance* New Jersey: Lawrence Erlbaum Associates Inc

Newman O (1972) *Defensible Space* New York: Macmillan

Schumacher EF (1973) *Small is Beautiful: a study of economics as if people mattered* London: Blond & Briggs

Sustainable Construction Task Group (2002) *Reputation, Risk and Reward* Garston: BRE

Sylvan R, Bennett D (1994) *The Greening of Ethics* Cambridge: White Horse Press

Vos JFJ (2002) Corporate Social Responsibility and the Modelling and Choice of Stakeholders *The 2002 International Sustainable Development Research Conference Proceedings* Shipley: ERP Environmental

Welford R (2000) *Corporate Environmental Management* London: Earthscan Publications Ltd

www.legislation.hmso.gov.uk

www.un.org

Chapter 3

Allan J (2001) Preserving Heritage or Revaluing Resources in Macdonald S, *Preserving Post-War Heritage*

Baldwin R, Yates A, Howard N, Rao S (1998) *BREEAM '98 for Offices* Garston: BRE

Baum A (1994) Quality and property performance *Journal of Property Valuation and Investment* 12 (1) 31–46

Baum A, Crosby N (1995) *Property Investment Appraisal* London: Routledge

Bebbington J, Gray R, Hibbitt C, Kirk E (2001) *Full Cost Accounting: an agenda for action* London: Association of Chartered Certified Accountants

Bowie N (1982) Who hoodwinked whom? 262 *Estates Gazette* 405

Brennan TP, Cannaday RE, Colwell PF (1984) Office Rent in the Chicago CBD *AREUEA Journal* 12:3 pp243–260

Brownhill D, Rao S (2002) *A Sustainability Checklist for Developments* Garston: BRE

Buchanan C (1963) *Traffic in Towns* London: HMSO

Bunyard P (1996) *Gaia in Action: Science of the Living Earth* Edinburgh: Floris Books

Capital Economics (2002) *Property in Business – a waste of space* London: RICS

Clift M, Bourke K (1999) *Study on whole life costing* Garston: CRC Ltd

Doane D, MacGillivray (2001) *Economic Sustainability of Staying in Business: a report for the Sigma project* London: New Economics Foundation

Donhead Audit Commission (2002) *Using Quality of Life Indictors* London: Audit Commission

English Heritage (2002) *The State of the Historic Environment Report 2002* London: English Heritage

Eversley D, Donnison D (1973) *London, Urban Patterns, Problems and Policies* London: CES

Eversley D (1971) Business News *The Sunday Times* 13 June

Forum for the Future (1996) *Programme for a Sustainable Economy* London: Forum for the Future

Galbraith JK (1994) *The World Economy Since the War* London: Sinclair-Stevenson

Galbraith JK (1958) *The Affluent Society* London: Hamish Hamilton

Galbraith JK (1996) *The Good Society* London: Sinclair-Stevenson

Hall P (1995) David Eversley Obituary – The urban warrior of planning *The Guardian* 1 July

Hawken P, Lovins AB, Lovins LH (1999) *Natural Capitalism: the next industrial revolution* London: Earthscan

Higginson S, Somer F, Terry A (2003) *Making Indicators Count: using Quality of Life Indicators in Local Government – identifying the missing link* London: New Economics Foundation and University of the West of England

Hoesli M, Macgregor B (2000) *Property Investment: Principles and Practice of Portfolio Management* Harlow: Longmans

Hutton W (2001) *Putting back the P in PLC* London: Industrial Society

Investment Property Databank (IPD) (2002) *The Investment Performance of Listed Buildings* London: IPD/English Heritage/RICS Foundation

Isaac D (1998) *Property Investment* Basingstoke: Macmillan

Jacobs J (1962) *The Death and Life of Great American Cities* London: Jonathan Cape

Klein N (2000) *No Logo: taking aim at the brand bullies* London: Flamingo/HarperCollins

Kincaid D (2002) *Adapting Buildings for Changing Uses* London: EF&N Spon

London First Sustainability Unit (2001) *A "Triple Bottom Line" for London, an index of London's sustainability* London: London First

Lovelock JE (1979) *Gaia: A New Look at Life on Earth* Oxford: Oxford University Press

McIntosh APJ (1997) *Towns and Cities – Competing for Survival* London: E&FN Spon

McWilliams D (1996) *London's Contribution to the UK Economy* London: Chamber of Commerce & Industry

Mishan EJ (1967) *The Costs of Economic Growth* London: Penguin

Mishan EJ (1972) *Elements of Cost Benefit Analysis* London: Unwin University Books

Mumford L (1961) *The City in History* London: Secker & Warburg

Revell JRS (1967) *The Wealth of the Nation* Cambridge: Cambridge University Press

Scanlon K, Edge A, Willmot T (1994) *The Listing of Buildings: the effects on value* University of Cambridge, The Royal Institution of Chartered Surveyors, English Heritage, Dept of Environment

RICS (2003) *RICS Appraisal and Valuation Standards* 5th Ed London: RICS

Salway F (1986) *Depreciation of Commercial Property* Reading: CALUS

Scanlon K, Edge A, Willmot T (1994) *The Economics of listed Buildings* Discussion Paper 43 University of Cambridge Department of Land Economy National Heritage

Shumacher EF (1973) *Small is Beautiful: a Study of Economics as if People Mattered* London: Blond & Briggs Ltd

Skidelsky R (1995) *The World after Communism* Basingstoke: Macmillan

Sustainability (2001) *Buried Treasure: uncovering the business case for corporate sustainability* London: Sustainability/UNEP

Sustainable Construction Focus Group (2000) *Towards Sustainable Construction: a strategy for the construction industry* London: The Construction Confederation

Sustainable Construction Task Group (2001) *Reputation, Risk and Reward* Garston: BRE

Thompson M (1979) *Rubbish Theory* Oxford: Oxford University Press

Vandell KD, Lane JS (1989) The economics of Architecture and Urban Design: some preliminary findings *AREUEA Journal* 17(2): 235–260

Von Weizsacker E, Lovins AB, Lovins LH (1997) *Factor Four Doubling Wealth – Halving resource Use* London: Earthscan

World Commission on Environment and Development (1987) *Our Common Future* Oxford: Oxford University Press

Zadek S, Tuppen C (2000) *Adding Values: the economics of sustainable business* London: BT occasional papers

www.commercialleasecodeew.co.uk

www.un.org

www.worldbank.org

Chapter 4

Anderson J, Howard N (2000) *The Green Guide to Housing Specification* Garston: BRE

Brand S (1997) *How Buildings Learn: What Happens After They're Built* London: Weidenfeld Nicolson Illustrated

Brownhill D, Rao S (2002) *A Sustainability Checklist for Developments* Garston: BRE

Building Research Establishment (2002) *BRE Information Paper 9/02: Refurbishment or Redevelopment of Office Buildings?* Garston: BRE

CABE and University College London [UCL] (2001) *The Value of Urban Design* London: Department of the Environment, Transport and the Regions [DETR]

Centre for Ecology & Hydrology, Lancashire University (undated) *Trees and Sustainable Urban Air Quality* accessed at www.es.lancs.ac.uk

Cope B, Garrington N, Matthews A, Watt D (1995) Biocide Residues as a Hazard in Historic Buildings *Journal of Architectural Conservation* 1(2)

Cox J, Fell D, Thurstain-Goodwin M (2002) *Red Man, Green Man* London: RICS Foundation

Curwell SR, March GG (1986) *Hazardous Building Materials* London: E&FN Spon

Department of the Environment [DoE] (1994) *Sustainable Development: the UK Strategy* London: HMSO

Department of the Environment (1994) *The Latham Report: 'Constructing the Team'* Final Report of the Government/Industry Review of Procurement and Contractual Arrangements in the UK Construction Industry London: HMSO

Department of Trade and Industry [DTI] (2003) *Our energy future – creating a low carbon economy* London: HMSO

Ecotech (2003) Roofing choice and the environment *Architecture Today* pp30–36 7 May

Edwards BW (1998) *Green Buildings Pay* London: E&FN Spon

English Heritage (2002) *State of the Historic Environment Report 2002* London: English Heritage

European Union (2002) *COM 0192 Directive on the Energy Performance of Buildings* at www.europa.eu.int/comm/energy/en/fa_2_en.html.

Girardet H (1991) *Creating Sustainable Cities* Totnes: Green Books

Goldsmith E (1972) *Blueprint for Survival* London: Houghton Mifflin Company

Harridge C, MacTavish A, McAllister I, Nicholson S (2002) *Guide to Sustainability Appraisal* London: Town and Country Planning Association

Hartland Thomas M (1947) *Building is Your Business* London: AllenWingate

Hawkens P, Lovins A, Lovins P (1999) *Natural Capitalism* London: Earthscan Publications Ltd.

Hewitt M (2001) Can trees cut pain *The Times* 4 September Section 2 p10

Hewitt M, Hagan S (2001) *City Flights* London: James & James Ltd

Horton C, Arnold D (2003). On-site factory speeds up prefabs *Building Design* May 23 p6

Howard N (1996) Embodied Energy and Consequential CO_2 in Construction *Proceedings of the 1996 International Symposium of CIBW67 on Energy and Massblown Buildings* Vienna: August

Jones P (2001) What next for waste? *Energy and Environmental Management* Nov/Dec

Lovelock J (1988[a]) *The Ages of Gaia* Oxford: Oxford University Press

Lovelock J (1979[b]) *Gaia: a new look at life on earth* Oxford: Oxford University Press

MaSC (2002) *Managing Sustainable Construction: Profiting from Sustainability* Garston: BRE

Meadows DH, Meadows DL, Randon J, Behrens W (1972) *The Limits to Growth A Report for the Club of Rome's Project on the Predicament of Mankind* New York: Universe Books

Mellet E (1999) *Sustainable Architecture* Rotterdam: NAI Publishers

Monteith JL (1973) *Principles of Environmental Physics* London: Edward Arnold

Morrell J (2001) *How to Forecast: a guide for business* Aldershot: Gower

Papanek V (1995) *The Green Imperative Ecology and Ethics in Design and Architecture* London: Thames & Hudson

Pearman H (2000) 2000 as "The Peacock House" *The Sunday Times* 26 March

Petty M (1995) There was something in the air *Cambridge Weekly News* 20 September

Pratt PL (1991) Keynote address to the Fifth International Conference on the Durability of Building Materials and Components Brighton Published in *Proceedings* London: E&FN Spon

Queensland Government *Ecologically Sustainable Office Fitout Guide* www.build.qld.gov.au

Risebero W (1992) *Fantastic Form* London: The Herbert Press

Redland Roofing Ltd (2002) *A Guide to Sustainable Roofing* Dorking: Redland Roofing Ltd

Rogers R (1985) *Observations on Architecture* London: Academy Editions

Rogers R (1999) *Final Report of the Urban Task Force: towards an urban renaissance* London: Spons Publishing Ltd

Rudlin D, Falk N (1999) *Building the 21st Century Home: the sustainable urban neighbourhood* London:

Butterworth Heinemann Ltd

Sayce S, Ellison L (2003[b]) Integrating sustainability into the appraisal of property worth: identifying appropriate indicators of sustainability *The American Real Estate and Urban Economics Association Conference, RICS Foundation Sustainable Development* Session August 21–23 Skye Scotland

Smith PF (2001) *Architecture in a Climate of Change: a guide to sustainable design* London: Architectural Press

Sudjic D (1986) *Norman Foster, Richard Rogers, James: New Directions in British Architecture* London: Thames & Hudson

Sustainable Construction Task Group (2002) *Reputation, Risk and Reward* Garston: BRE

Taylor GD (2000) *Materials in Construction* Harlow: Longman

The Natural Step (2002) Silicon Valley Toxics Coalition 2002 www.svtc.org

Thomas R (Ed) (2003) *Sustainable Urban Design* London: Spon Press Ltd

Vale B, Vale R (1991) *Towards a Green Architecture* London: RIBA Publications

Wastebusters Ltd (Eds) *The Green Office Manual* (2000) London: Earthscan Publications Ltd

Webb R (2002) The Architects Journal Product Focus *The Architects Journal* Spring p10

Williams A (2001) Back to the Future *Architects Journal* 31 May

Williamson T, Radford A, Bennetts H (2003) *Understanding Sustainable Architecture* London: Spon Press Ltd

www.bre.co.uk

www.carmtechnology.co.uk

www.cbpp.org.uk

www.es.lancs.ac.uk

www.homezonenews.org.uk

www.iea.org

www.ipcc..ch

www.nher.co.uk

www.securedbydesign.com

www.svtc.org

www.vauban.de

www.segalselfbuild.co.uk

Chapter 5

DETR (1999[a]) *A Better Quality of Life: A Strategy for Sustainable Development for the UK* London: HMSO

DETR (1999[b]) *Quality of Life Counts* London: HMSO

DETR (2000) *Our Towns and Cities: The Future, Delivering the Urban Renaissance* London: HMSO

Henriques A, Raynard P (2001) *Social Sustainability Research Theme* R&D report for the Sigma Project

Investment Property Databank (IPD) (2002) *The Investment Performance of Listed Buildings* London: IPD/RICS

Klein N (2000) *No Logo* London and New York: Picador

Sayce S, Ellison L (2003[a]) Towards Sustainability Indicators for Commercial Property Occupiers and Investors published in *Proceedings of the International Sustainable Development Research Conference* March 24–25 Shipley: ERP

Sayce S, Ellison L (2003[b]) *Integrating Sustainability into the Appraisal of Property Worth: identifying indicators of sustainability* Paper to the American Real Estate and Urban Economics Association Conference August 21–23 Skye

Scanlon K, Edge A, Wilmot T (1994) *The Listing of Buildings: the effect on value* London: RICS, English Heritage, Department of National Heritage, University of Cambridge

Sustainable Construction Task Group (2002) *Reputation, Risk and Reward* Garston: BRE

Weizsacker, E (1997) *Factor Four: Doubling Wealth, Halving Resource Use* London: Earthscan

www.amec.com

www.cgnu.co.uk

www.europa.eu.net

www.acca.com

www.defra.gov.uk

www.investis.com

www.naturalstep.org.

www.accountAbility.com

www.csrnetwork.com

www.hdr.undp.org

Chapter 6

Anderson J, Mills K (2002) *Refurbishment or redevelopment of office buildings? Sustainability comparisons* Garston: BRE

Beauregard RA, Haila A (2000) The Unavoidable Continuities of the City pp22–36 in Marceuse P, van Kemper R (2000) *Globalizing Cities: a new spatial order?* Oxford: Blackwell Publishers Ltd

Bell S, Morse S (1999) *Sustainability Indicators* London: Earthscan

Brand S (1997) *How Buildings Learn* 2nd Ed. London: Phoenix Illustrated

Currie D, Scott A (1991) *The Place of Commercial Property in the UK Economy* London: London Business School

Elkin T, McLaren D, Hillman M (1991) *Reviving the City: towards sustainable urban development* London: Friends of the Earth

Hall P (1996) *Cities of Tomorrow* Oxford: Blackwells

Hawken P, Lovins AB, Lovins LH (1999) *Natural Capitalism: the next industrial revolution* London: Earthscan Publications Ltd

Henneberry J (1996) Property Market Structure and Behaviour: the interaction of use and investment sectors and its impact on Urban and Regional Development *RICS Cutting Edge Research Conference* University of the West of England September

Insignia Richard Ellis (2002) Economic Arguments For Tall Office Buildings, a Memorandum by Insignia Richard Ellis to the Select Committee on Transport, Local Government and the Regions

Massey D, Catalano A (1978) *Capital and Land: Landownership by Capital in Great Britain* London: Edward Arnold Ltd

Mellet E (1999) *Sustainable Architecture* Rotterdam: NAI Publishers

O'Neill G (1999) *My East End* London: Penguin Books

Pine J, Gilmore J (1999) *The Experience Economy* Boston Mass: Harvard Business School Press

Plender J (1982) *That's the Way the Money Goes* London: Andre Deutsch

Walker A, Sayce S, McIntosh A (2001) *Buildings: a new life an interim report to DTI* London: Kingston University/DLG Architects and King Sturge

Soja E (1989) *Post-modern Geographies* London: Verso Books

Sustainable Development Commission (2001) *State of Sustainable Development in the UK: Improving eco-efficiency* Sustainable Development Commission, Preparatory Report 14

van Kempen R (2000) *Globalizing Cities: a new spatial order* Oxford: Blackwell Publishers Ltd

www.officescorer.info

www.sustainability-checklist.co.uk

General bibliography

Anderson J, Howard N (2000) *The Green Guide to Housing Specification* Garston: BRE

Building Research Establishment [BRE] (2002) *BRE Information Paper 9/02: Refurbishment or Redevelopment of Office Buildings?* Garston: BRE

CABE and University College London [UCL] (2001) *The Value of Urban Design* London

Cope B, Garrington N, Matthews A, Watt D (1995) Biocide Residues as a Hazard in Historic Buildings *Journal of Architectural Conservation* 1(2)

Cox J, Fell D, Thurstain-Goodwin M (2002) *Red Man, Green Man* London: RICS Foundation

Curwell SR, March GG (1986) *Hazardous Building Materials* London: E&FN Spon

Department of the Environment [DOE} (1994) *The Latham Report 'Constructing the Team' Final Report* of the Government/Industry Review of Procurement and Contractual Arrangements in the UK Construction Industry London: HMSO

Department of the Environment [DoE] (1994) *Sustainable Development: the UK Strategy* London: HMSO

Department of the Environment Transport and the Regions [DETR] (1999[a]) *A Better Quality of Life: A Strategy for Sustainable Development for the UK* London: HMSO

Department of the Environment Transport and the Regions [DETR] (1999[b]) *Quality of Life Counts* London: HMSO

Department of the Environment Transport and the Regions [DETR] (2000) *Our Towns and Cities: The Future, Delivering the Urban Renaissance* London: HMSO

Department of Trade and Industry [DTI] (2003) *Our energy future – creating a low carbon economy* London: HMSO

Ecotech (2003) Roofing choice and the environment *Architecture Today* 7 May pp30–36

European Union (2002) *COM 0192 Directive on the Energy Performance of Buildings* at www.europa.eu.int/comm/energy/en/fa_2_en.html.

Eversley D (1971) Business News *The Sunday Times* 13 June

Girardet H (1991) *Creating Sustainable Cities* Totnes: Green Books

Goldsmith E (1972) *Blueprint for Survival* London: Houghton Mifflin Co

Hall P (1996) *Cities of Tomorrow* Oxford: Blackwells

Harridge C, MacTavish A, McAllister I, Nicholson S (2002) *Guide to Sustainability Appraisal* London: Town & Country Planning Association

Investment Property Databank (IPD) (2002) *The Investment Performance of Listed Buildings* London: IPD/RICS

Hewitt M (2001) Can trees cut pain? *The Times* 4 September Section 2 p10

Hewitt M, Hagan S (2001) *City Flights* London: James & James Ltd

Hopkins M (2003) *The Planetary Bargain: Corporate Social Responsibility Matters* London: Earthscan Publications Ltd

Horton C, Arnold D (2003) On-site factory speeds up prefabs *Building Design* May 23 p6

Lovelock J (2000[a]) *The Ages of Gaia* Oxford: Oxford University Press

Lovelock J (2000[b]) *Gaia: a new look at life on earth* Oxford: Oxford University Press

Margolis JD, Walsh JP (2001) *People and Profits? The Search for a Link Between a Company's Social and Financial Performance* New Jersey: Lawrence Erlbaum Associates Inc

Monteith JL (1973) *Principles of Environmental Physics* London: Edward Arnold

Morrell J (2001) *How to Forecast: a guide for business* Aldershot: Gower

Parnell P, Sayce S (1999) 'Attitudes towards financial incentives for green buildings' Kingston University School of Surveying and Drivers Jonas Property Consultants

Pearce D (1993) *Blueprint 3: Measuring Sustainable Development* London: Earthscan

Pearman H (2000) 2000 as "The Peacock House" *The Sunday Times* 26 March

Petty M (1995) There was something in the air *Cambridge Weekly News* 20 September

Pine J, Gilmore J (1999) *The Experience Economy* Boston Mass: Harvard Business School Press

Plender J (1982) *That's the Way the Money Goes* London: Andre Deutsch

Pratt PL (1991) Keynote address to the Fifth International Conference on the Durability of Building Materials and Components Brighton published in *Proceedings* London: E&FN Spon

Queensland Government Ecologically Sustainable Office Fitout Guide www.build.qld.gov.au

Redland Roofing Ltd (2002) *A Guide to Sustainable Roofing* Dorking: Redland Roofing Ltd

RICS (2003) *RICS Appraisal and Valuation Standards* 5th Ed London: RICS

Risebero W (1992) *Fantastic Form* London: The Herbert Press

Rogers R (1985) *Observations on Architecture* London: Academy Editions

Rudlin D, Falk N (1999) *Building the 21st Century Home: the sustainable urban neighbourhood* London: Butterworth Heinemann Ltd

Sayce S, Ellison L (2003[a]) Towards Sustainability Indicators for Commercial Property Occupiers and Investors Published in *Proceedings of the International Sustainable Development Research Conference* March 24–25 Shipley: ERP

Smith PF (2001) *Architecture in a Climate of Change: a guide to sustainable design* London: Architectural Press

Sudjic D (1986) *Norman Foster, Richard Rogers, James: New Directions in British Architecture* London: Thames & Hudson

Sustainable Construction Focus Group (2000) *Towards Sustainability – a strategy for the construction industry* Birmingham: CIP Ltd

Taylor GD (2000) *Materials in Construction* Harlow: Longman

The Natural Step (2002) Silicon Valley Toxics Coalition 2002 www.svtc.org

Thomas R (Ed) (2003) *Sustainable Urban Design* London: Spon Press Ltd

Vale B, Vale R (1991) *Towards a Green Architecture* London: RIBA Publications

Walker A, Sayce S, McIntosh A (2001) *Buildings: a new life an interim report to DTI* London: Kingston University/DLG Architects and King Sturge

Wastebusters Ltd (Eds) (2000) *The Green Office Manual* London: UK Earthscan

Williams A (2001) Back to the Future *Architects Journal* 31 May

www.accountAbility.com

www.amec.com

www.bre.co.uk

www.carillionplc.com

www.carmtechnology.co.uk

www.cbpp.org.uk

www.cgnu.co.uk

www.commercialleasecodeew.co.uk

www.csrnetwork.com

www.defra.gov.uk

www.europa.eu.net

www.ftse4good.com

www.hdr.undp.org

www.homezonenews.org.uk

www.investis.com

www.iea.org

www.ipcc..ch

www.legislation.hmso.gov.uk

www.naturalstep.org.

www.nher.co.uk

www.officescorer.info

www.securedbydesign.com

www.segalselfbuild.co.uk

www.sloughestates.com

www.sustainability-checklist.co.uk

www.sustainability-index.com

www.svtc.org

www.un.org

www.un.org

www.un.orgwww.acca.com

www.vauban.de

www.worldbank.org

www.legislation.hmso.gov.uk

Index